CIVIL WAR BATTLEFIELDS

THEN & NOW

Thunder Bay Press
An imprint of the Baker & Taylor Publishing Group
10350 Barnes Canyon Road, Suite 100, San Diego, CA 92121
www.thunderbaybooks.com

Produced by Salamander Books,
a division of Pavilion Books Group,
1 Gower Street, London WC1E 6HD, UK

Library of Congress Cataloging-in-Publication Data

Campi, James.
  Civil War battlefields then & now / James Campi Jr.
      p. cm.
  "Completely revised and updated with all new text and modern
photographs"--Publisher.
  ISBN-13: 978-1-60710-583-1
  ISBN-10: 1-60710-583-7
1. United States--History--Civil War, 1861-1865--Pictorial works. 2. United
States--History--Civil War, 1861-1865--Battlefields--Pictorial works. 3. United
States--History--Civil War, 1861-1865--Battlefields. 4. United States--History--
Civil War, 1861-1865--Campaigns. 5. Historic sites--United States. 6. Historic
sites--United States--Pictorial works. 7. Repeat photography--United States.
I. Title. II. Title: Civil War battlefields then and now.
  E468.7.C27 2012
  973.70022'2--dc23
                    2012020655

Dedication
To my wife, Jennifer

Acknowledgments
This book would not have been possible without the yeoman's work done by historians
of Civil War photography in the past few decades. They have taken upon themselves
the monumental task of sifting through old stereoviews and glass plates to document
the visual record of the war. In particular, I am indebted to William A. Frassanito, whose
books on Civil War photography, *Gettysburg: A Journey in Time*; *Antietam: The Photographic
Legacy of America's Bloodiest Day*; *Grant and Lee: The Virginia Campaigns 1864-1865*; and
Early Photography at Gettysburg have created an entire generation of buffs who scour Civil
War battlefields looking for the exact spot where wartime photographs were taken.
I also referred to William C. Davis's six-volume study, *The Image of War 1861-1865*,
originally published by the National Historical Society, which is a masterpiece of Civil
War history and photography. Finally, I would be remiss if I failed to mention the
Center for Civil War Photography, a nonprofit organization devoted to the study of
Civil War photography and photographers. The Center has produced numerous fine
publications replete with Civil War images and history.

In addition, I want to thank the photographers who contributed to the contemporary
images in this book: Garry Adelman, Charlie Crawford, Robert Schenk, Mark Campi
and Steve Stanley. I also want to thank Frank Hopkinson, who patiently worked with
me to select the photographs and write the text of the book. Also, thank you to Mary
Koik, who reviewed the text of the book. Finally, I want to thank my wife Jennifer for
indulging my interest in the war and who traveled with me to capture many of the
"now" images

Picture Credits
The publisher wishes to thank the following for kindly providing the photographs for
this book.

Then photographs
Corbis: pages 8 and 88.
Getty Images: pages 10, 11, 18, 78, and 82.
Library of Congress: pages 9, 10, 11, 12, 13, 14, 16, 17, 18, 19, 20, 21, 22, 23, 24, 25, 26,
27, 28, 29, 30, 31, 32, 33, 34, 36, 37, 38, 39, 40, 41, 42, 43, 44, 45, 46, 47, 48, 49, 50, 52, 53,
54, 55, 56, 57, 58, 59, 60, 62, 63, 64, 65, 66, 67, 68, 69, 70, 71, 72, 74, 75, 76, 77, 79, 81, 83,
84, 85, 86, 87, 89, 90, 91, 92, 93, 94, 95, 97, 98, 99, 100, 101, 102, 103, 104, 105, 107, 108,
109, 110, 111, 112, 113, 114, 115, 116, 117, 118, 119, 121, 122, 123, 124, 125, 126, 127,
128, 130, 131, 132, 133, 134, 135, 136, 137, 138, 139, 140, 141, 143, and 144.
Massachusetts Commandery Military Order of the Loyal Legion and the U.S. Army
Military History Institute: pages 80, 96, and 120.
The Manassas Museum, VA: page 45.

Now photographs
All photos Anova Image Library with the following exceptions:
Gary Adelman: pages 91 and 93.
James Campi, Jr.: pages 11, 17, 23, 29, 33, 37, 45, 47, 49, 59, 61, 63, 95, 105, 129, 131,
135, and 137.
Mark Campi: pages 71 and 77.
Charlie Crawford: pages 107, 109, and 115.
Library of Congress: pages 27, 31, 65, 67, 87 113, and 135.
Simon McBurney: page 69.
Alexander Mitchell IV: pages 15, 35, 39, 47, 97, 99, 101, 103, and 133.
Robert Price: pages 9, 79, 81, 83, 89, 111, 121, and 125.
Steve Stanley: page 143.
David Watts: pages 25, 27, 41, 43, 53, 55, 73, 75, and 141.

Printed in China
2 3 4 5 6 18 17 16 15 14

CIVIL WAR BATTLEFIELDS

THEN & NOW

JAMES CAMPI JR.

THUNDER BAY
P·R·E·S·S

San Diego, California

CIVIL WAR BATTLEFIELDS
THEN & NOW INTRODUCTION

More than 150 years have passed since Confederate guns first fired on Fort Sumter. The resulting two-day artillery duel over possession of this small masonry fort in Charleston Harbor signaled the beginning of the Civil War, the greatest conflict in U.S. history. For four long years, North and South clashed in 10,000 battles and skirmishes that defined America as a nation. More than 625,000 soldiers and 50,000 civilians perished in the war.

Seven generations later, the Civil War continues to capture the imagination of Americans for many reasons. The war is often referred to as the last old-fashioned war and first modern war, and certainly the struggle contained elements of both. Because of the enormous number of men enlisted in the Union and Confederate armies, millions of today's Americans can trace their ancestry back to the war. And, unlike in earlier conflicts, many of the men in blue and gray were prolific writers, so thousands of eyewitness accounts of the war survive as an invaluable resource for historians.

However, it is the photography of the Civil War that most often fascinates enthusiasts of the war today. Photography made the Civil War the first conflict in which noncombatants far from the battlefield could see for themselves the misery and carnage of war. Obscure landmarks such as the Stone House at Manassas and the Devil's Den at Gettysburg were reproduced as newspaper woodcuts and brought to life at photography exhibitions.

For the first time as well, civilians had an opportunity to view haunting photographs of the battlefield casualties. Unlike the practice used in previous conflicts, these stark images were neither romanticized nor glorified by a painter's brush. Referring to Mathew Brady's photographs of the dead at Antietam, an unknown *New York Times* reporter wrote, "Mr. Brady has done something to bring to us the terrible reality and earnestness of the war. If he has not brought bodies and laid them in our door-yards and among our streets, he has done something very like it." These photographs of human wreckage jolted the public consciousness in a manner similar to how television images of the Vietnam War did so a century later.

When the Civil War began, photography was still in its infancy and consisted mostly of portraiture. Brady, America's most celebrated photographer at the time, was renowned for the large "imperial" portraits that hung in his comfortable New York and Washington, D.C., galleries. With the coming of war, Brady switched gears and focused much of his attention on images taken from "the seat of war." His teams of photographers followed the armies through all four years of the conflict. When in the field, Brady often placed himself in the camera's view, and his pointed beard and pince-nez glasses are familiar sights in his wartime images. But, the war that made Brady a legend left him penniless and led to the closure of his once-famous galleries.

Despite the omnipresence of the Brady name on Civil War–era photographs, Brady rarely if ever took any battlefield photographs. Instead he left that task to his talented assistants, the most prominent of whom were Alexander Gardner, the manager of Brady's Washington gallery, and James F. Gibson. It was this pair, rather than Brady, who took the images of the dead at Antietam. Later, the two were joined by another photographer, Timothy O'Sullivan, to take a series of equally dramatic photos at Gettysburg. By that time, Gardner had parted with Brady and set up his own gallery in Washington.

In addition to these gentlemen, several other photographers earned their reputations during the war. Captain Andrew Russell was assigned by Union general Herman Haupt to document the engineering innovations of the Union army, as well as to photograph the battlefields. George N. Barnard, another Brady associate, became the official photographer of the Union armies in the Western theater. Many of Barnard's photos of General William T. Sherman's campaign through Georgia and the Carolinas appear in the latter pages of this book.

The Confederates boasted several wartime photographers as well, although the scarcity of materials for both making and reproducing photographs in the blockade-starved South hampered their efforts. One of the first images of the war, showing the Stars and Bars of the Confederacy flying proudly over Fort Sumter, was taken by F. K. Houston of Charleston. Arguably the best-known Confederate photographer was another Charlestonian, George S. Cook, whose image of a Union shell bursting inside battered Sumter is one of the war's most noteworthy.

These early pioneers in the profession of war photography were able to invoke powerful emotions with their images of the people, places, and events of the Civil War. In fact, so powerful were the photographs that, in the years immediately following the war, Americans tried to put both the war and its photographs behind them. The images—and the memories they conjured up—were simply too painful. Many of the images and original glass plates were lost, some winding up as glass for greenhouses. Fortunately, in the decades after the war, the federal government realized the enormous historical significance of the photos. They purchased the bankrupt Brady's remaining photos for $25,000 and began accumulating other wartime images as well. In addition, other historically minded organizations, such as the Massachusetts Commandery of the Military Order of the Loyal Legion, amassed large collections of photographs from the Civil War period. Today, many of these images are preserved at the Library of Congress, the National Archives, and the U.S. Army Military Institute in Carlisle, Pennsylvania, where they will remain to captivate and fascinate future generations.

The Capitol, Washington, D.C., 1861

Arlington House, Near Alexandria, VA, 1861

Centreville, VA, 1862

Federal Occupation of Fort Pulaski, GA, 1862

Drewry's Bluff, VA, 1862

Union Mills, VA, 1862

Fredericksburg, VA, 1862

Sunken Road, Fredericksburg, VA, 1863

John Burns House, Gettysburg, PA, 1863

Little Round Top, Gettysburg, PA, 1863   p. 74

Captured Cannon, Vicksburg, MS, 1863   p. 82

Lookout Mountain, TN, 1864   p. 92

Massaponax Church, Spotsylvania, VA, 1864   p. 98

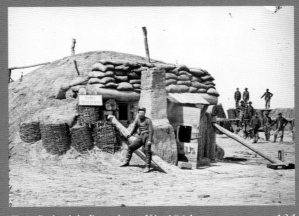

Fort Sedgwick, Petersburg, VA, 1864   p. 104

Occupation of Atlanta, GA, 1864   p. 114

State Capitol, Nashville, TN, 1864   p. 118

Charleston, SC, 1865   p. 126

Pennsylvania Avenue, Washington, D.C., 1865   p. 138

FORT SUMTER, CHARLESTON, SC
The capture of Fort Sumter was the flash point that sparked the four-year conflict

THE SURRENDER OF FORT SUMTER

The surrender of Fort Sumter—viewed here in the distance from the Confederate-built Fort Johnson—galvanized the North. Prior to the bombardment, there existed strong sentiment in the Northern states to allow the "erring sisters to go in peace." However, the unprovoked attack on Fort Sumter dramatically changed the situation. The response to President Abraham Lincoln's call for 75,000 men to put down the rebellion was overwhelming. Untrained but enthusiastic volunteers flocked to recruiting stations, and the small Union army became a force to be reckoned with practically overnight. Envelope covers, like the one shown here, reflected these early patriotic sentiments.

More than two generations of bitter sectional controversy exploded into armed conflict on April 12, 1861, when Confederate guns fired on Fort Sumter. Ironically, no one was killed during the bombardment. Only after the guns fell silent were two Union soldiers injured firing a salute, making them the first casualties of America's bloodiest war. A few hours later, the Stars and Bars of the Confederate states were unfurled over Fort Sumter. Today, Fort Sumter (pictured above) little resembles the three-tiered brick and masonry structure that once dominated Charleston Harbor. The North and the South expended lives and resources liberally in often-desperate attempts to hold or capture the fort, which was a symbol for both sides. By the end of the war, the fort's walls had been leveled by a sustained Union siege. Where the Confederate flag once flew, only the ruins of the first-tier gun rooms remain.

FAR LEFT: The bombardment that unleashed the four-year Civil War did little damage to the masonry walls of Fort Sumter. However, the heated projectiles fired by the Confederates—known as "hot shot"—set wooden structures within the fort ablaze. In the 1861 image of the fort, the Stars and Bars of the South fly over one of the gutted structures inside the fort.

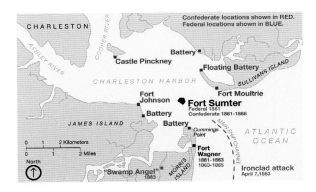

THE CAPITOL, WASHINGTON, D.C.
Lincoln made certain that his seat of government was safe from enemy disruption

After the surrender of Fort Sumter, attention turned to the respective capitals of the two nations. Washington, D.C., became a city under siege, with Confederate batteries on the Potomac effectively blockading the district. Government buildings were turned into barracks, and Union troops were quartered in the Capitol Rotunda, beneath its unfinished dome. Throughout the war, Lincoln would be extremely sensitive about the defense of Washington, depriving the field armies of troops so that the city's forts were adequately manned.

ABRAHAM LINCOLN

The election of Abraham Lincoln as president was the catalyst for secession. Lincoln, a self-taught country lawyer with little legislative or military experience, was thrust into the most perilous position ever faced by an American chief executive. Little more than a month after his inauguration in March 1861, he was confronted by a rebellion within sight of the White House. The length of the conflict and fear of foreign intervention would cause him to issue the Emancipation Proclamation, freeing the slaves in the rebelling states and leading to total emancipation in 1865. It would take time, but eventually Lincoln found commanders like Ulysses S. Grant and William T. Sherman to see the war through to victory. He again showed his greatness toward the end of the war, with his conciliatory approach to reuniting the nation. Unfortunately, his plans for an easy peace were shattered by an assassin's bullet on April 15, 1865.

In the early days of the war, there was some discussion about discontinuing the renovation of the U.S. Capitol and its enormous new cast-iron dome (right). Lincoln would have none of this defeatist talk. He ordered the construction work to continue, as a "symbol that the Union would go on." Four years later, in March 1865, Lincoln would be inaugurated to a second term beneath a completed dome and its crowning feature, the bronze statue *Freedom*.

ABOVE LEFT: Washington, D.C., was an armed camp for the duration of the war. The city was the most fortified capital in the world by the war's end. Protecting the approaches to the city was particularly important; pictured here is a Union artillery unit unlimbered along railroad tracks that crossed the Potomac into Virginia.

OLD CAPITOL PRISON / SUPREME COURT, WASHINGTON, D.C.

The building that had been a makeshift capitol in 1814 gained a new role in 1861

Prior to the war, Washington was considered a Southern city, with slavery permitted within its limits. As a result, the Union capital was crawling with Confederate sympathizers, many longing for the day when their compatriots across the river would force the Lincoln administration to flee. Many of these sympathizers did more than just long for liberation; several turned to spying as a method of ensuring the defeat of the Northerners in their midst. In response to the threat of espionage, Lincoln suspended the writ of habeas corpus and threw several suspected rebel spies into the Old Capitol Prison, located on the current site of the U.S. Supreme Court.

ROSE O'NEAL GREENHOW

Rose O'Neal Greenhow was one of the most celebrated spies of the Civil War. At a young age, she became a Washington, D.C., socialite, mingling with presidents, lawmakers, and high-ranking military leaders. She was close to Southern rights advocate John C. Calhoun, a senator from South Carolina who heavily influenced her politics. When the war broke out, Greenhow quietly created a network of spies, using her contacts in Congress and the military to gather information. Her crowning achievement was a message she sent to Confederate general P. G. T. Beauregard, warning him of the Union army's advance on Manassas. Following the battle, she was thrown into the Old Capitol Prison, eventually being deported through the lines to Richmond. She died in 1864, drowning while trying to escape a blockade runner that had been run aground by the Union navy.

Among the notables incarcerated within the prison's walls was Rose O'Neal Greenhow, the spy who warned the Confederate army of the Union march on Manassas. Her warning enabled the Southern army to concentrate its forces south of Bull Run. The Old Capitol Prison, which had been both a boardinghouse and school before the Civil War, played a significant role in the war's aftermath but was razed in 1867.

ABOVE: The Old Capitol Prison was initially replaced by a row of brick houses. These were pulled down to make way for the Supreme Court Building, designed by Cass Gilbert and completed in 1935.

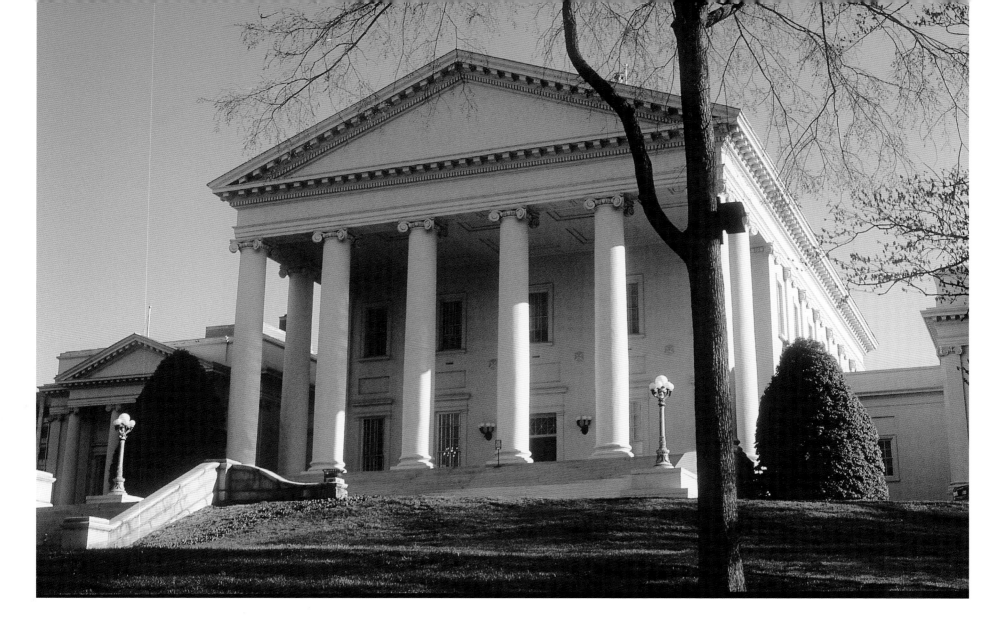

CONFEDERATE CAPITOL, RICHMOND, VA

Thomas Jefferson's elegant building witnessed many rancorous debates throughout the war

Ninety miles south of Washington, the new Confederate government was establishing itself in the manufacturing center of Richmond, Virginia. Representatives from thirteen Southern states gathered in the stately Virginia Capitol, designed by Thomas Jefferson in 1788. As the war dragged on, the Capitol was the scene of rancorous debates over the handling of the war, the first conscription in America, and the enlistment of slaves in the war's waning days.

Richmond became the symbol of Southern resistance. During the early days of the conflict, Northern newspaper editors declared that the city must be captured before the Confederate Congress was able to congregate in Richmond. Throughout the war, "On to Richmond" would be a rallying cry for the Union army in the East. Although enlarged by the addition of two new wings, the former Confederate Capitol appears today much as it did during the war.

CONFEDERATE WHITE HOUSE, RICHMOND, VA

Confederate president Jefferson Davis based his government here for four years, before fighting forced evacuation in 1865

JEFFERSON DAVIS

Jefferson Davis resigned from the U.S. Senate on January 21, 1861. The Southern statesman had advised his colleagues against secession, but felt it was his duty to follow his native Mississippi out of the Union. A West Point graduate and Mexican War veteran, Davis had hoped for a high rank in the fledgling Confederate army. But the representatives meeting in Montgomery, Alabama, to create a new Southern government selected Davis as the first president of the Confederate States of America in February 1861. Three months later, Davis moved the Confederate capital from Montgomery to Richmond, Virginia. In April 1865, the Confederate government was forced to flee Richmond when the Union army broke the Southern defenses at nearby Petersburg. Davis was captured on May 10, 1865, and imprisoned at Fort Monroe. He was released two years later and died at his home in Mississippi in 1889.

Although gray rather than white, the Confederate executive mansion was referred to as the "White House of the Confederacy." Within these walls, the proud and often difficult Jefferson Davis presided over the Southern experiment in nationhood. Davis often met with his cabinet and generals in this three-story building. It was here that Davis met with his most successful commander, Robert E. Lee, to plan the ill-fated Gettysburg campaign.

As the war dragged on, the Confederate White House became something of a refuge for President Davis from the bitter denunciations of his many critics. When the city was evacuated in 1865, the house served as the Union army's headquarters, and President Abraham Lincoln briefly sat at Davis's desk. While the house itself has been restored to its wartime appearance, the one-time executive mansion is now overshadowed by the medical college campus of Virginia Commonwealth University (below).

ABOVE: The Confederate White House at the corner of Twelfth and Clay Streets in the Court End neighborhood of Richmond was built in 1818. It survived the bombardment and fire of 1865, and by the time of this photograph in 1901 it was already functioning as a Confederate museum.

ARLINGTON HOUSE, NEAR ALEXANDRIA, VA

Robert E. Lee's former home was an unlikely backdrop to one of Mathew Brady's most famous photos

President Lincoln's immediate concern was the security of his own capital. Just across the Potomac in Virginia, the new Southern banner could be seen waving defiantly. To prevent the shelling of the White House and other public buildings, in early May 1861 the Union army marched across the Potomac to seize Arlington Heights. Arlington House, the home of Robert E. Lee, was occupied and served as a Union army headquarters. Arlington House, begun in 1802, was not left unscathed by the Union occupation. Lee's wife Mary was the daughter of George Washington's step-grandson and only heir, and the house contained many Washington heirlooms that were eventually claimed by the Federal government.

ABOVE: Throughout the war, Arlington House was a popular subject for photographers. Pictured here are Union soldiers standing along the portico.

BELOW: General Irwin McDowell, commander of the Union army at First Manassas, is pictured with his staff on the steps of Arlington House. Following his defeat at First Manassas, he served as a corps commander until he was relieved after the debacle at Second Manassas in 1862.

By 1864, the Union quartermaster general chose the Arlington House property as the location of a cemetery for those who died in the war. Although it had been seized for nonpayment of taxes, Custis Lee, an heir, sued the government after the war and was awarded $150,000 for the title to the land. Today, more than 320,000 American soldiers and their families are buried there. Arlington House has been preserved and restored as the Robert E. Lee Memorial.

MATHEW BRADY

Mathew Brady was one of the pioneers of American photography. He became a practitioner of the new art at an early age and eventually opened studios in New York and Washington. He experimented with new types of photography and was best known for his portraits of prominent Americans and celebrities. When the war erupted, it became Brady's goal to record images of the conflict. His fading eyesight meant that much of the fieldwork was done by other photographers, among them Alexander Gardner and Timothy O'Sullivan. However, Brady's gift for marketing meant he received the lion's share of the publicity and credit. He also placed himself in many of the photos and is seen at the center of the main photo (opposite) wearing a top hat. After the war, financial difficulties left him bankrupt. He died penniless in New York City in January 1896.

MARSHALL HOUSE, ALEXANDRIA, VA
Scene of the death of a Union colonel and the making of a Federal hero

FRANCIS BROWNELL

The death of Colonel Elmer Ellsworth brought national attention to young Francis Brownell, a private in the Eleventh New York Volunteer Infantry Regiment, also known as the Fire Zouaves. On May 24, 1861, Brownell joined Ellsworth as he entered the Marshall House, guarding the stairs while Ellsworth pulled down the Confederate flag. As Ellsworth and Brownell descended the stairs, they were confronted by shotgun-wielding James Jackson, the owner of the hotel. Brownell attempted to knock aside the gun, but not before Jackson shot Ellsworth in the chest. After a short struggle, Brownell avenged his commander by bayonetting Jackson. For his actions, Brownell was promoted to second lieutenant. Sixteen years later, he received the Medal of Honor for his actions that day.

Although the Northern troops sent across the Potomac did not encounter any Confederate forces, the Union occupation of Arlington Heights and nearby Alexandria was not entirely bloodless. As Union colonel Elmer Ellsworth rode into Alexandria at the head of his New York Fire Zouave Regiment, he spotted the rebel colors flying from the Marshall House, a local hotel. Ellsworth marched into the hotel, determined to make the banner his first war trophy.

Ellsworth did not leave the Marshall House alive. He grabbed the flag, but as he walked down the steps, he was shot dead by the hotel's proprietor, who was in turn killed by one of Ellsworth's men. As the North's first martyr, Ellsworth's body was laid in state in the White House. His men threatened to burn down the Marshall House, but the hotel survived the war. Today a Holiday Inn occupies the site.

SLAVE DEALERS, ALEXANDRIA, VA
Alexandria was a key railway hub and also the center of the Virginia slave trade

The port of Alexandria was one of the oldest cities in Virginia, with close ties to George Washington and other Founding Fathers. Mount Vernon was located nearby, a historic site sacred to both the North and South. As the first occupied Southern city, it was an early target for photographers. They recorded several images of a structure unknown to most Northern audiences—a slave pen, with cells for slaves about to be sold—on Duke Street in downtown Alexandria. Alexandria was the state's main slave-trading center; Franklin & Armfield, another slave-trading company on Duke Street, remained in business until the town was seized in May 1861. Price, Birch & Company's slave pens were subsequently used to imprison troublesome Union soldiers.

ABOVE: For the sick and wounded of the Union army in the East, Alexandria was a safe haven. Railroads made it a convenient location for hospitals and convalescent camps, similar to the one pictured here.

RIGHT: A Virginia historical marker now stands outside the former Alexandria slave pen, now known as Freedom House. The structure was first used to confine slaves by Franklin & Armfield, at one time the largest slave-dealing firm in the South.

Occupied Alexandria was the hub for Union operations in the East throughout the war. The city was the terminus of the Orange and Alexandria Railroad, which connected strategic towns in northern and central Virginia. The railroad became one of the principal supply lines for the Union, transporting men and munitions southward, and the sick and wounded back to the city's crowded hospitals. Far too many wound up buried in the rapidly expanding Alexandria National Cemetery.

LEFT: Although the Union war effort was frequently stymied by poor leadership on the battlefield, it benefited from outstanding minds in the manufacturing and industrial sector. Among them was Herman Haupt, an engineer and West Point graduate who managed U.S. Military Railroads for two crucial years in 1862 and 1863. Haupt's genius for organization kept the Union railroads in the East operating at full throttle. His crews repaired bridges and railroads in record time. An independent thinker, Haupt eventually resigned rather than tolerate interference from his superiors.

SUDLEY CHURCH, FIRST MANASSAS, VA

In July 1861, a stream was all that separated the opposing sides; the bluecoats crossed it near this country chapel

FIRST BULL RUN/FIRST MANASSAS

The first major land battle of the Civil War is remembered by two distinct names: Northerners referred to the battle as First Bull Run; Southerners called it First Manassas. The difference in names reflects the penchant Northerners exhibited throughout the war to identify battles with rivers and creeks. Their Confederate counterparts tended to name battles after nearby localities. Regardless of the name, the battle was a morale-boosting victory for the Confederates. Today, the battlefield is preserved as Manassas National Battlefield Park. The above photo shows a Federal cavalry at Sudley Ford in March 1862.

In mid-July 1861, the Union army around Washington began moving south toward the vital rail junction of Manassas. The Confederate army, lined up behind a meandering stream called Bull Run, prepared to meet them. The Union commander, Brigadier General Irwin McDowell, eschewed a front assault against the rebel lines and instead launched an attack against their left flank. The bluecoats crossed Bull Run near a country chapel known as Sudley Church.

As the Union troops marched past Sudley Church toward the sounds of battle, the small chapel became a hospital. Soon the numbers became overwhelming, and many of the wounded were laid out in the yard. More than 300 wounded Union soldiers were captured in and around the church at the end of the battle. The church was so badly damaged during the war that it was razed to the ground. The current church was built in 1922.

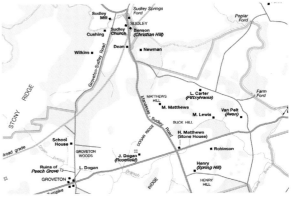

STONE HOUSE, MANASSAS, VA
This insignificant country tavern served both sides on the Manassas battlefield

HENRY HOUSE HILL

The turning point of the Battle of First Manassas occurred on Henry House Hill, so designated because of a house on the height owned by Judith Henry. Henry was eighty-five and bedridden at the time of the battle, unable to seek shelter with the rest of her family. As the armies struggled for control of the hill, Confederate sharpshooters firing from the house made it an inviting target. Henry became a casualty of Union counterfire, and is now buried in the family cemetery adjacent to the postwar structure built to replace the house destroyed in the battle. The famous stand of General Thomas J. Jackson and his Virginia brigade on Henry House Hill turned the tide of the battle and earned both the general and the brigade the sobriquet "Stonewall."

One of the most prominent landmarks on the Manassas battlefield is the Stone House, a country tavern located on the Warrenton Turnpike near its junction with Sudley Road. The seemingly victorious Union army surged past the house on July 21, 1861, as it attempted to finish off the remnants of the Confederate army on nearby Henry House Hill. As with most battlefield structures, the tavern was soon filled with the wounded.

It was not long before the Union troops were marching past the Stone House again, this time in defeat. The house was soon captured by Virginian troops with fixed bayonets. One year later, the house witnessed another battle—and another Northern defeat. Following the Battle of Second Manassas, the tavern was used by the Confederates to parole Union prisoners. Even today, the house still bears the scars of the two battles.

CENTREVILLE, VA

In spite of extensive fortification and fake ordnance, Confederate forces eventually abandoned the area around Manassas Junction

After the Battle of First Manassas, a lull descended upon the combatants. The Union army returned to Washington to lick its wounds and build a more formidable force, soon designated the Army of the Potomac. Meanwhile,

the victorious Confederate legions settled into camps around Centreville, where they remained until March 1862. The Southerners also commenced building an extensive network of entrenchments to protect Manassas Junction.

ABOVE AND TOP RIGHT: Nineteenth-century Centreville is nearly unrecognizable today, and the once-sleepy crossroads village has been consumed by commercial development. The old stone church in the foreground of the wartime image survives; since 1973, it has housed an Anglican Catholic congregation.

Despite the earthworks and fortifications at Centreville, the Confederate army was in a precarious position, vulnerable to Union offensives in the valley and down the Potomac River. The rebel commander, Joseph E. Johnston, was particularly concerned about the exposed position. In March 1862, he evacuated Centreville and Manassas, destroying millions of dollars' worth of foodstuffs and other matériel vital to Confederate survival. Except for a brief period during the summer of 1862, Centreville remained in Union hands for the rest of the war.

QUAKER GUNS

Following the Battle of First Manassas, the Confederate army commenced building a series of earthworks around Centreville. From a distance, the fortifications appeared so formidable that Union general George B. McClellan opposed attacking the fearsome defenses. However, he need not have worried. The Southerners did not have the heavy ordnance necessary to make the works impregnable. To compensate for their lack of real weapons, the inventive Southerners painted logs to look like cannons. These faux cannons (pictured above and left in an abandoned Centreville fort) were dubbed "Quaker guns" by the chagrined Northern press. Today, one of the remaining forts, known as the Mayfield Fort, includes a replica Quaker gun.

FORT PULASKI, GA

An early victory in the Union's bid to gain control of the coastline and waterways

Elsewhere, after the Battle of First Manassas, the opposing forces were on the move. In the West, Union soldiers liberated most of Kentucky and began a campaign to gain control of the Mississippi River. Along the coast, the Union navy strengthened its blockade of rebel ports, secure in the knowledge that the infant Confederate navy could offer little resistance. Combined with the army, the two services were able to restore Federal control over key coastal waterways.

One of the first Union victories along the Atlantic coastline was at Fort Pulaski, a bastion guarding the Savannah River. The masonry fort, designed in part by then-Lieutenant Robert E. Lee, was considered nearly invulnerable. However, in April 1862, a young Union engineer named Quincy Gilmore set out to prove rifled cannons had made masonry forts obsolete. The damage done to the fort by Gilmore's guns can still be seen today.

LEFT AND ABOVE: The damage done to Fort Pulaski by Quincy Gilmore's rifled guns marked the end of masonry forts in warfare. Ultimately, Gilmore was able to breach the brick walls of the fort, exposing the garrison's powder magazine and making surrender inevitable.

LEFT AND BELOW LEFT: The wartime image of Fort Pulaski, taken soon after the bombardment, illustrates the immense damage done to the fort. The breach is visible in the center of the photo on the left. The image below left shows an interior casement, and demonstrates how the brick was pounded into rubble by Union artillery.

FEDERAL OCCUPATION OF FORT PULASKI, GA
With Pulaski under control, the Union began its slow asphyxiation of Confederate coastal defenses

ABOVE: A lone sentinel guards one of the Union cannons in captured Fort Pulaski. The Cockspur Island lighthouse is visible in the distance.

ABOVE: Another image of the Union forces that occupied Fort Pulaski after its capture. In the foreground is a Union cannon named after the governor of Rhode Island, William Sprague. The fort's demilune moat can be seen in the background.

The once-mighty Fort Pulaski began to crumble under the unrelenting bombardment of 1862. In less than two days, several casemates were destroyed, and Pulaski's southeast wall was breached, making the fort vulnerable to attack by a Union assault party. Even worse, the breach meant that enemy gunners were able to fire directly upon the fort's powder magazine. Faced with the likely destruction of both the fort and its defenders, Fort Pulaski's commander chose to surrender.

The fort's surrender was a major blow to Southern independence. Its capture allowed the Union navy to tighten its blockade and permitted the Union army to gradually gain control of key islands off the Georgia and South Carolina coasts. For the remainder of the war, Fort Pulaski would be held by Union troops bored by the tedium of garrison duty. Today Fort Pulaski has been restored to its wartime appearance by the National Park Service.

ST. PETER'S CHURCH, NEW KENT, VA

The setting for George Washington's wedding provided shelter for the Union army more than a hundred years later

In April 1862, the Army of the Potomac began another campaign toward Richmond. Not overland past the now-abandoned Confederate earthworks at Manassas but by sea, toward the peninsula between the York and James Rivers. The Union army, numbering in excess of 100,000 men, began moving slowly up the peninsula toward the colonial port of Yorktown. As the Union host approached Yorktown, their advance was abruptly halted by a handful of Confederate gunners. Rather than risk his men in an assault against the Southern lines, Major General George McClellan laid siege to Yorktown. He brought up heavy artillery, including the ten thirteen-inch mortars of Battery 4, manned by men of the First Connecticut Heavy Artillery.

In May 1862, the Confederate commander, General Joseph Johnston, abandoned Yorktown and began retreating closer to Richmond. McClellan's army followed, eventually catching up with its adversaries at Williamsburg on May 5. After a sharp rearguard action, the pursuit continued, with the Southern forces finally halting within sight of the spires of Richmond. The Union army began settling in for a siege, taking over several local buildings in the process. One of the local structures commandeered by the Union army was St. Peter's Church, the site of George

Washington's wedding in 1759 (seen here at left and below). During the Peninsula Campaign, the church was strategically located between the Chickahominy River and the Union base at White House, Virginia. The church grounds served as a bivouac for the Union Second Corps commander. Two years later, in June 1864, Union and Confederate cavalry clashed nearby. Although damaged, the church survived the war.

BATTLE OF WILLIAMSBURG

The Battle of Williamsburg was an unintended consequence of General Joseph E. Johnston's retreat up the peninsula to Richmond. At Williamsburg, the vanguard of the Army of the Potomac caught up with the rear of Johnston's army, ensconced behind a line of hastily built earthworks east of Williamsburg. The resulting battle enhanced the reputations of two up-and-coming Union generals, Joseph Hooker and Winfield Scott Hancock. They led the Union assaults at Williamsburg, with Hancock later repulsing a disjointed Confederate counterattack toward the end of the day. Following the battle, under cover of darkness, the Southerners continued their dispiriting retreat toward Richmond.

DREWRY'S BLUFF, VA
Rebel gunners inflicted considerable damage on Union ships from this fort on the James River

THE USS *MONITOR*

The USS *Monitor* was perhaps the most groundbreaking invention of the Civil War. Although not the first ironclad warship, it was certainly the most innovative. Its inventor, Swedish-born engineer John Ericsson, introduced the first armored turret—a creation quickly emulated by the world's navies. The *Monitor*'s duel with the larger and more heavily armed CSS *Virginia* made the *Monitor* a legend throughout the North. However, its low profile and top-heavy gun arrangement made the vessel unseaworthy in the open ocean. The *Monitor* foundered off Cape Hatteras in December 1862.

BELOW: Today, an interpretative display pinpoints the exact location of the historical photo.

While the Union army moved up the peninsula toward Richmond in 1862, "Uncle Sam's webbed feet" were also busy trying to open the waterborne route to Richmond. Five Union gunboats, including the famous ironclad USS *Monitor*, began steaming up the James River toward the Confederate capital. The *Monitor*'s counterpart, the CSS *Virginia* (formerly the *Merrimack*), had recently been scuttled, and little stood in the way of the Union task force and Richmond.

However, a handful of Confederate naval gunners, including the survivors of the *Virginia*, were determined to make a stand at a recently built fort at Drewry's Bluff on the James. On May 15, 1862, the *Monitor* and its consorts were halted by the plunging fire from Drewry's Bluff. One ship, an experimental ironclad named the *Galena*, was riddled by rebel gunfire. Today Drewry's Bluff is protected by the National Park Service as part of Richmond National Battlefield Park.

CHICKAHOMINY RIVER BRIDGE, VA

Robert E. Lee's first offensive maneuver as Confederate commander was a resounding success

For more than a month, the armies eyed one another across the lines outside Richmond. Except for the inconclusive Battle of Seven Pines (May 31–June 1, 1862), the opposing forces spent most of their time bridging rivers, bringing up reinforcements, and preparing for battle. Behind the gray lines, the new Confederate commander, General Robert E. Lee, was making plans to lift the siege. His strategy would make use of the Chickahominy River, which split the Federal army in two.

GENERAL ROBERT E. LEE

General Robert E. Lee is one of the most celebrated military leaders in American history. A career army officer, he served with distinction during the Mexican War. Shortly after the Civil War began, he was offered command of the Union army but declined because he could not bear taking up arms against his native Virginia. After assuming command of the Army of Northern Virginia in June 1862, Lee initiated a series of campaigns that twice brought the war to the North. His victories at Second Manassas, Fredericksburg, and Chancellorsville made him an idol to his troops. In 1864, Lee successfully managed to hold off the vastly superior Union army and forced them into a siege at Petersburg. In April 1865, Lee's dwindling army was finally overwhelmed, resulting in his surrender at Appomattox. After the war he served as a college president, and died in Lexington, Virginia, in 1870.

On June 26, 1862, Lee attacked north of the Chickahominy, catching McClellan's army off guard and forcing it to retreat. McClellan was compelled to evacuate his positions north of the river, destroying the bridges his engineers had constructed over the past four weeks. The damage to Grapevine Bridge would delay Major General Thomas "Stonewall" Jackson's pursuit long enough to enable the Union army to flee intact. Grapevine Bridge has since been replaced by a modern structure (above).

LEFT: Grapevine Bridge across the Chickahominy River was of great strategic importance in early 1862. Built by members of the Fifth New Hampshire Regiment at the end of May to facilitate McClellan's advance on Richmond, it was destroyed by the retreating Union army just one month later.

CEDAR MOUNTAIN, VA
Stonewall Jackson's soldiers fought a fierce battle against a smaller force of Union men that threatened Richmond from the north

Following Lee's success lifting the siege of Richmond, the focus of the war in Virginia moved to Culpeper County. A new Union army, designated the Army of Virginia and commanded by General John Pope, began moving southward along the Orange and Alexandria Railroad. By August 1862, the Federals had occupied Culpeper and were threatening Richmond from the north. To counter this threat, Lee sent Stonewall Jackson to the scene to suppress Pope's forces.

ABOVE: Officers of the Tenth Maine Volunteer Infantry Regiment, posing on the Cedar Mountain battlefield in an image taken by Timothy O'Sullivan. Veterans of the regiment would later dedicate a monument to their Cedar Mountain dead in nearby Culpeper National Cemetery.

On August 9, 1862, Jackson attacked Pope's divided army at Cedar Mountain. Despite outnumbering their adversary two to one, Jackson's men were nearly driven from the field. At one point, the fighting became so desperate that Jackson was forced to draw his sword in order to rally his men—the only time during the war he would do so. Today, 152 acres of historic Cedar Mountain are protected by the Civil War Trust.

GENERAL CHARLES S. WINDER

Maryland native Charles S. Winder was one of Stonewall Jackson's favorite lieutenants. Winder participated in the bombardment of Fort Sumter as a major of artillery. In March 1862, he was promoted to brigadier general and given command of Jackson's beloved Stonewall Brigade. Later, his performance would earn him a promotion to divisional command. He played a prominent role in Jackson's 1862 campaigns from the Shenandoah Valley to Cedar Mountain. At Cedar Mountain, despite illness and being carried to the battlefield in an ambulance, Winder insisted on leading his division in battle. He was horribly mangled by an artillery shell early in the battle, and was taken to this rural homestead to die. His body was later transported to Richmond to lie in state in the Confederate capitol.

STONE BRIDGE, MANASSAS, VA
Fighting returned to an unrecognizable battlefield at Manassas in 1862, where a Confederate trap produced a second Union defeat

ABOVE: The Stone Bridge across Bull Run was one of the most prominent features of the Manassas landscape. This image was taken by photographer George Barnard after the Confederate withdrawal from Manassas in March 1862.

In the wake of Cedar Mountain, the armies again returned to Manassas, although it little resembled its bucolic appearance during the first skirmish in July 1861. Months of Confederate encampment, followed by Union occupation, had wreaked havoc on the battlefield. Few trees or fences remained, having been consumed for campfires or used as building materials, and many of the bridge crossings had been destroyed by retreating Southerners, only to be repaired by their Northern counterparts.

For three days in late August 1862, fighting raged just west of the Stone Bridge. General Pope, convinced he had Stonewall Jackson trapped, threw his army piecemeal against Jackson's line along an old abandoned railroad cut. In reality, it was Pope who had unwittingly stepped into a trap—a trap sprung when General James Longstreet's Confederate troops smashed into Pope's left flank, resulting in a defeat nearly as humiliating as at First Manassas. The Stone Bridge across Bull Run was built in 1825. Its location on the turnpike between Alexandria and Warrenton made it a structure of critical strategic importance. The bridge was the scene of a diversionary attack by Union forces during the Battle of First Manassas, and was destroyed during the Confederate evacuation of March 1862. A temporary wooden span was built at the site in time for Second Manassas, but it was demolished by retreating Union forces at the end of August. A stone bridge similar to the original was constructed in 1884 and is now a popular feature on the battlefield landscape.

UNION MILLS, VA

Throughout the war rebel cavalry, and later guerrilla units, succeeded in disrupting transportation networks

The maneuvering of the armies wreaked havoc on the transportation network in Virginia. The Orange and Alexandria Railroad was a particular favorite of rebel cavalry raiders, who would disrupt Federal supplies by burning its numerous bridges.

Later in the war, when the regular Confederate cavalry was no longer able to penetrate into northern Virginia, guerrilla units such as Colonel John Mosby's partisan rangers would continue to prey on the railroad.

BELOW: The railroad bridge at Union Mills remained a priority for both armies throughout the war. This image shows Union troops guarding the rebuilt structure. Note the damaged blockhouse in the background, a victim of the endless Confederate raids on the Orange and Alexandria Railroad.

The railroad bridge across Bull Run seemed to get more than its share of attention. Despite numerous precautions, including the construction of a blockhouse, the bridge at Union Mills was destroyed and rebuilt seven times during the war. Only the efficiency of Union colonel Herman Haupt's repair crews enabled the trains to keep supplying the Yankee army.

BELOW: A modern railroad bridge now spans Bull Run at Union Mills, although wartime stone abutments remain. The site is accessible by trails from nearby Hemlock Overlook Regional Park.

LOST COMMUNITY

At the time of the Civil War, Union Mills was an important railroad stop on the Orange and Alexandria Railroad. Its name derived from mills built in the area at the end of the nineteenth century. Its location near the railroad crossing of Bull Run meant that both armies put considerable effort into fortifying the region. After the war Union Mills was unable to compete with nearby Clifton and went into gradual decline. Little remains today, although mill races and several of the Confederate forts are still visible.

HARPERS FERRY, WV

The garrison here was a target for Confederate forces who achieved a dramatic but short-lived victory

Scenic Harpers Ferry, situated at the confluence of the Potomac and Shenandoah Rivers, was once described by an admiring Thomas Jefferson as "worth a voyage across the Atlantic." In 1859 abolitionist John Brown attacked the U.S. Arsenal at Harpers Ferry, with the intent of arming Virginia's slaves. Although unsuccessful, Brown's attempt to foment a slave rebellion inflamed passions on both sides, making a compromise between the North and South impossible.

It was not Harpers Ferry's beauty but its strategic importance that captured the attention of Robert E. Lee in September 1862. As the Confederate Army of Northern Virginia moved northward into Maryland, Lee and Stonewall Jackson developed plans to capture the Union garrison at Harpers Ferry. Today, Harpers Ferry is protected by the National Park Service, including many of the nineteenth-century buildings visible across the Potomac in the modern photograph.

ABOVE: Like so many rail bridges in the Civil War, the one crossing the Potomac at Harpers Ferry did not survive the conflict.

ABOVE: The Twenty-second New York was a frequent subject of photographers at Harpers Ferry in 1862. This image, taken by Mathew Brady, shows soldiers on Maryland Heights.

THE CAPTURE OF HARPERS FERRY

The capture of Harpers Ferry was critical to Robert E. Lee's invasion plans in September 1862. His goal of maneuvering in Maryland and Pennsylvania could not be accomplished with the Union garrison threatening his communications with Virginia. Lee dispatched Stonewall Jackson to subdue the Federals occupying the town. Jackson seized control of the heights encircling Harpers Ferry, ensnaring the Union army in a trap from which they could not escape. More than 12,500 Yankees were forced to capitulate, the largest mass surrender in U.S. Army history until World War II.

OLD HAGERSTOWN PIKE, ANTIETAM, MD

The bloodiest day in American history was also the first time war dead were documented in photographs

ALLAN PINKERTON

Allan Pinkerton (seen here on the left, with Abraham Lincoln and Major General John A. McClernand) is best remembered for creating the famous Pinkerton Detective Agency in Chicago in the 1850s. Pinkerton's agency built its reputation solving railroad robberies and counterfeiting rings. It was while working in this capacity that Pinkerton first met George McClellan and Abraham Lincoln. During the early years of the war, Pinkerton was an advisor to both men on military intelligence matters. McClellan used Pinkerton to determine Confederate army strength; unfortunately, the numbers he provided were vastly overstated. At one point he credited the Army of Northern Virginia with three times the number of soldiers actually present for duty. Pinkerton's erroneous information fed McClellan's cautious nature and contributed to his hesitancy to attack on the peninsula and in Maryland. Pinkerton left Federal service after Antietam, returning to his detective agency in Chicago. He died in 1884.

LEFT: Alexander Gardner's team was able to photograph the Confederate dead at Antietam just one day after Lee's retreat southward across the Potomac. This image shows Southerners killed along the Hagerstown Pike near the West Woods. The Hagerstown Pike appears to the right between the fence lines; a rural farm lane is located on the left of the photo.

As the guns fell silent at Harpers Ferry, a far more devastating clash was brewing along Antietam Creek near Sharpsburg, Maryland. The Battle of Antietam, fought on September 17, 1862, would be the bloodiest day in American history. The two sides inflicted 22,000 casualties on each other over the course of the day, including as many as 4,700 dead or mortally wounded.

Antietam was also the first battle in history in which the dead of the battlefield were substantially photographed. Some of the first photographs were taken beside the old Hagerstown Pike, where fighting raged in the early morning hours that day. In this vicinity, Stonewall Jackson's command struggled against repeated attacks by three separate Union army corps. Today the site is protected as part of Antietam National Battlefield.

DUNKER CHURCH, ANTIETAM, MD

Union troops managed to rescue their men and avoid significant losses in spite of a fierce attack

One of the most prominent features on the Antietam battlefield was the church of a German Baptist sect that baptized its members by total immersion—hence the nickname "Dunker Church." In an effort to extricate bluecoats caught in the early fighting on September 17, 1862, Union general John Sedgwick's

Second Corps Division launched an attack toward the Dunker Church. The assault turned into a deadly trap as Confederate troops launched almost simultaneous assaults against both of Sedgwick's flanks.

Despite the fierceness of the attacks against Sedgwick, the division retired in good order. The Second Corps historian would later note that "not a color is left to become a trophy of that bloody fight." The bullet-scarred Dunker Church also survived the battle, only to fall prey to Mother Nature in 1921. However, the church's bricks were saved and became part of a new Dunker Church, rebuilt in time for the battle's centennial in 1962.

"BLOODY LANE," ANTIETAM, MD

Sustained attacks on Confederate forces during a day of heavy fighting filled this sunken road with bodies

The Battle of Antietam was fought in phases that reflected the piecemeal attacks ordered by McClellan, the Union commander defeated by Lee a few months earlier on the Virginia peninsula. The focus of the second phase of the battle, fought by elements of the Second Corps, was a sunken country road that Confederates under General Daniel Harvey Hill were using as a makeshift entrenchment. The repeated assaults against the road would forever earn it the moniker "Bloody Lane."

BELOW: On September 19, 1862, Alexander Gardner and his team took several images of the Confederate dead in Bloody Lane. The Union attack on Bloody Lane crossed the rolling landscape in the background.

STEREOSCOPIC VIEWS OF BATTLE

Many scenes from the conflict were reproduced as stereoscopic cards that could be placed in a viewer to give an almost three-dimensional view of the battle scenes. Publishers charged thirty cents a view and felt they had to justify their prices, as evidenced below.

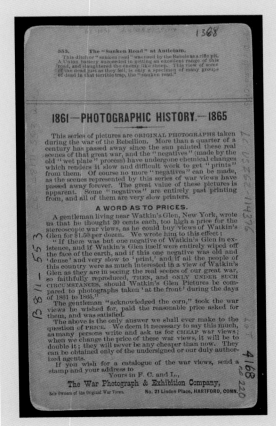

For four hours, Southern troops staved off their counterparts in blue. The repeated charges gradually thinned the Confederate ranks, and the sunken road became filled with the dead and wounded. Eventually, the Union assault broke the rebel line, opening a path to Lee's rear. However, the exhausted Northerners failed to grasp the opportunity. Today the once blood-soaked lane is dotted with markers and monuments that tell the tale of the struggle waged there.

RIGHT: In another image by Gardner, Dr. Anson Hurd of the Fourteenth Indiana Volunteer Infantry is attending the wounded at one of the many field hospitals established in the days following the Battle of Antietam.

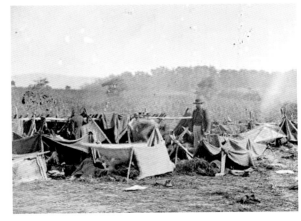

BURNSIDE BRIDGE, ANTIETAM, MD

Ambrose Burnside's inability to take a stone bridge quickly stalled the Union attack

GENERAL AMBROSE BURNSIDE

General Ambrose Burnside (pictured here reading a newspaper opposite photographer Mathew Brady in 1864) was a fixture in the Union high command throughout the war. His success along the North Carolina coast in early 1862 led to his appointment to corps command. His performance at Antietam suggested he had been promoted beyond his competence, yet Lincoln selected him as commander of the Army of the Potomac in the wake of McClellan's dismissal. His tenure as army commander marked the nadir of Union fortunes in the East. He would eventually serve as a corps commander under Grant during the Overland Campaign of 1864, and was dismissed after his failure at the Battle of the Crater in July of that same year.

BELOW: The stone wall along the eastern bank of Antietam Creek became a makeshift cemetery after the battle. Pictured here are wooden grave markers of Union dead. Their remains would later be moved to Antietam National Cemetery.

The final phase of the battle was fought over a triple-arched stone bridge across Antietam Creek. Here, Union general Ambrose Burnside's command was confronted by a handful of Georgian troops positioned on a bluff overlooking the bridge. Despite the enormous numerical superiority of the Federal forces, it took Burnside nearly four hours to capture the bridge and the heights beyond. The bridge is today known as "Burnside Bridge."

After the capture of the bridge that bears his name, victory lay within Burnside's grasp. However, rather than seize the opportunity, Burnside dawdled for two hours, giving Lee time to bring up badly needed reinforcements. The repulse of Burnside's belated attack brought the Battle of Antietam to an end. Two days later, Lee withdrew his battered but intact army across the Potomac, ending his first invasion of the North.

FREDERICKSBURG, VA

Despite arriving first, General Burnside's hesitation meant the enemy took the town while Federal troops watched

After Antietam, the armies gradually moved south toward the Rappahannock River. In November 1862, the Army of the Potomac, now under the command of Burnside, began a movement down the north bank of the Rappahannock toward Fredericksburg. Although most historians consider him to have been a mediocre general, Burnside was actually able to steal a march on Lee, arriving at Fredericksburg well before any Southerners arrived to defend it.

The bridges into Fredericksburg were destroyed, but the Rappahannock was fordable at several points. There was nothing stopping the Union host from taking the town—except the fears of the commander on the scene, who was worried that his troops would be trapped on the south side of the river in the event of a sudden storm. The result was that the Union troops simply sat on the north bank watching their gray-clad enemy march into Fredericksburg unopposed.

ABOVE RIGHT: A panoramic view of Fredericksburg, taken in March 1863 by Timothy O'Sullivan. The image was captured from the northern bank of the Rappahannock River, from the site of the boyhood home of George Washington. Today, trees obscure this view of Fredericksburg.

LEFT: Many of the views associated with the Battle of Fredericksburg were taken after the battle, in the spring of 1863 and 1864. One of the most compelling images was captured in 1863 by A. J. Russell, who photographed Confederate soldiers posing on the remains of the Richmond, Fredericksburg, and Potomac Railroad bridge. To the left of the bridge are the Excelsior Mill and a tobacco factory, used as a Confederate military hospital earlier in the war.

LACY HOUSE, FREDERICKSBURG, VA

Serving as Union headquarters as well as a hospital, this fine mansion survived heavy bombardment as well as two battles

One of the finest views of Fredericksburg could be found at Chatham, the Georgian mansion owned by Confederate major J. Horace Lacy. The house served as headquarters for a multitude of Union generals throughout the war. During the Battle of Fredericksburg, the house was headquarters for the Federal army's Right Grand Division. After the battle, the mansion became a hospital where poet Walt Whitman and Red Cross founder Clara Barton both served as nurses.

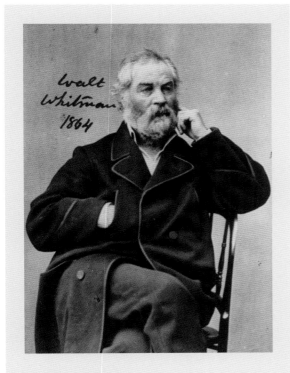

WALT WHITMAN

Renowned poet and journalist Walt Whitman was forty-two years old when the Civil War began. During the early days of the war he wrote feature articles for the *Brooklyn Standard* and *New York Leader*. After learning that his brother George was wounded at Fredericksburg, he traveled south to find his sibling. His journey took him to Chatham, where he witnessed the horrors of war for the first time. The wounded men, amputated limbs, and horrible sanitary conditions inspired him to become a nurse, assisting Union doctors in the area for the next month. Afterward, he joined the U.S. Christian Commission and continued his work ministering to the wounded for the remainder of the war. His wartime experiences encouraged him to write the poetry collection *Drum-Taps* as well as *Memoranda During the War*.

On December 11, 1862, Burnside attempted to cross the Rappahannock on pontoon bridges located just below Chatham. After the bridge builders were repeatedly fired upon by snipers on the south bank, Burnside ordered a bombardment of the town. The mansion shook from the recoil of siege guns planted on Chatham's front lawn. The house survived the battle, as well as a second attack against Fredericksburg in May 1863. It became part of the national park in 1975.

ABOVE: Today, stately Chatham Manor serves as the headquarters of the Fredericksburg and Spotsylvania National Military Park. Exhibits inside the building tell the story of Fredericksburg, the Lacy family, and Chatham during the Civil War. Outside, visitors are treated to outstanding views of modern Fredericksburg.

SUNKEN ROAD, FREDERICKSBURG, VA
Hidden from sight, Confederate soldiers inflicted heavy losses on Union forces during their repeated assaults

Although he had stationed sharpshooters in Fredericksburg, Lee had no intention of defending it. Instead, he placed most of his army south of the town, roughly parallel to the Richmond, Fredericksburg, and Potomac Railroad. The remainder were drawn up at the foot of Marye's Heights, in a sunken road invisible to the Union forces massing in the town. This photo (left) was taken in May 1863, immediately following the Union occupation of Marye's Heights during the Second Battle of Fredericksburg.

The North Carolina and Georgia men defending the sunken road on December 13, 1862, were lined up six ranks deep in some places. As the Union lines drew nearer, the Confederates unleashed volley after volley on the unprotected bluecoats. Fifteen Union brigades made assaults against the trench, resulting in more than 8,000 Federal casualties. Today the remains of the sunken road are located beside the Fredericksburg Battlefield Visitor Center.

BROMPTON, FREDERICKSBURG, VA

Originally built by a French family, for a time this house proved vital to the defense of the Confederate line

Towering behind the sunken road is Marye's Heights, named for a French Huguenot family that settled there and built Brompton, the Marye family mansion. During the battle of December 13, 1862, Marye's Heights was occupied by massed Confederate artillery. These guns blasted the waves of blue infantry attempting to seize the trench. According to one rebel gunner, "A chicken could not live on that field when we open on it."

ABOVE AND LEFT: Brompton was a popular subject for photographers after the Battle of Fredericksburg. Damage to the exterior of the home is clearly visible in both images. In the above photo, earthworks constructed by the Confederate army are seen in the foreground.

Five months later, during the Second Battle of Fredericksburg, Marye's Heights was again the key to the Confederate defense. This time, however, the Union troops were able to break the thinly held rebel line. Today, Brompton is the residence of the president of the University of Mary Washington, a school closely associated with the battlefield. South of the mansion is the Fredericksburg National Cemetery, where 16,000 Union soldiers now rest, many of them killed in the attempts to take the heights.

MARYE'S HEIGHTS

One of the few images that captured the Union perspective of Marye's Heights was taken in 1864, likely by photographer A. J. Russell. The photograph shows the bloody plain crossed by Federal soldiers during multiple assaults on the sunken road and the heights beyond. A storm of shells and small-arms fire rained down on this area during the December 13, 1862, fighting. In the background, just above the brick building that dominates the foreground of the image, are the columns of Brompton.

HAZEN MONUMENT, STONES RIVER, TN

Named for Colonel William Hazen, this was one of the first Civil War memorials

While the North was recovering from Burnside's debacle at Fredericksburg, another battle was brewing in central Tennessee. On December 31, 1862, the Confederate Army of Tennessee struck the right flank of the Army of the Cumberland northwest of Murfreesboro. Despite the collapse of the Union flank, the line held, thanks in part to the stand of Colonel William Hazen's brigade. Hazen's men held the Round Forest—a critical portion of the Union line—against four assaults.

FEMALE COMBATANTS

Although both the Union and Confederate armies forbade the enlistment of female soldiers, it is estimated that several hundred served in uniform disguised as men. The inadequacy of army medical examinations, coupled with the large number of underage boys in the ranks, enabled women to conceal their gender. Among the females who served was Frances Clalin Clayton, who joined a Missouri artillery unit to be with her husband, Elmer Clayton. Calling herself "Jack Williams," she fought in several battles, including Fort Donelson and Stones River. It is not known for certain why she ultimately left the army; many believe she revealed her true identity after the death of her spouse at Stones River.

After the pummeling the Union army received, Confederate commander General Braxton Bragg assumed his opponent would retreat. Instead, General William Rosecrans maintained the Union position, enticing Bragg to make an ill-considered assault in the late afternoon of January 2, 1863.

The next day, Bragg began a withdrawal to Tullahoma, leaving Rosecrans in command of the field. Today much of the Stones River battlefield is protected, including the Hazen Brigade monument—one of the first memorials erected to honor Civil War soldiers.

CHANCELLORSVILLE, VA

The trap that failed to snare Lee and Jackson

In April 1863, the nation's eyes again turned to Virginia, where the Army of the Potomac was preparing an offensive against Lee's army. The Union forces, now under the command of General Joseph Hooker, boldly swept across two rivers to reach the rear of the Confederate army. Concentrating his forces at the sleepy crossroads of Chancellorsville, Hooker was certain that he had forced Lee into a trap from which he could not escape.

Unfortunately for Hooker, Lee and Jackson were not so easily snared. On May 2, 1863, Jackson's corps marched around the Union army, striking Hooker's right flank. The surprise assault transformed the Union line into a mass of fleeing men groping their way through the tangled second-growth forest. However, the thick woodland and oncoming darkness confused the Southerners as well. That evening, Jackson was mortally wounded by his own men. He died one week later. A monument was erected close to the place where he fell.

ABOVE: This image of the 110th Pennsylvania Volunteer Infantry Regiment was taken by A. J. Russell on April 24, 1863, just a few days before the beginning of the Chancellorsville campaign. Nine days later, the regiment was decimated in fighting near the Chancellorsville crossroads.

GENERAL THOMAS J. JACKSON

General Thomas J. Jackson was one of the most enigmatic commanders of the Civil War. Prior to the war, he was a professor of artillery and natural philosophy at the Virginia Military Institute. The stand of his brigade on Henry House Hill during First Manassas earned him the nickname "Stonewall." In May 1862, when the Confederate cause seemed nearly lost, he launched a campaign in the Shenandoah Valley that is still required reading in military academies around the world. During the year that followed, Jackson became Lee's most trusted lieutenant, serving with distinction at Second Manassas, Antietam, and Fredericksburg. In May 1863, Jackson's flank attack at Chancellorsville turned certain defeat into victory for the South. His death dealt a devastating blow to Confederate hopes for independence.

SEMINARY RIDGE, GETTYSBURG, PA
Well placed to observe troop movements on the roads into Gettysburg, this seminary served both sides during the war

The Southern victory at Chancellorsville notwithstanding, the Confederate cause looked bleak in June 1863. Large parts of Tennessee were occupied, and the Confederacy's last bastion on the Mississippi was under siege. It fell upon Lee's army to revive Confederate fortunes. In early June, he ordered the Army of Northern Virginia toward the Potomac and Pennsylvania. On July 1, elements of his army clashed with Union cavalry on the rolling hills outside Gettysburg.

LEFT: One of the most memorable photos taken after the Battle of Gettysburg depicts three captured Confederate soldiers on their way to prison camps in the North. The image was taken by Mathew Brady on Seminary Ridge, a week or two after the battle. The log breastworks upon which they pose were constructed by their compatriots on July 4, 1863, in preparation for a Union counterattack that was never launched.

The twelve roads that enter Gettysburg attracted the two armies like magnets. On the morning of July 1, 1863, thousands of soldiers in blue and gray were converging on the town. The Confederate lines advanced upon McPherson Ridge, only to be thrown back by Union reinforcements. On Seminary Ridge, the Lutheran Theological Seminary served as an observation post and makeshift hospital—first for the Union army, and later for the Confederates.

ABOVE: Today, the Lutheran Theological Seminary at Gettysburg maintains an active postgraduate campus on Seminary Ridge. Its most prominent feature, Schmucker Hall, is now a museum and library maintained by the Adams County Historical Society.

JOHN BURNS HOUSE, GETTYSBURG, PA

Confederate soldiers overwhelmed Union lines on McPherson Ridge, but John L. Burns survived his wounds to become a national hero

JOHN BURNS

John Lawrence Burns, the "Old Patriot," became one of the most popular subjects for photographers in the days and weeks following the battle. Burns is pictured here, recuperating from his wounds, in an image by Brady. The flintlock rifle he carried into battle leans against the wall. Born in 1793, Burns was a veteran who had fought in the War of 1812 and the Mexican-American War of 1846–48. At the age of sixty-seven, he volunteered to fight in the Civil War but was rejected as being too old. He was sent to Gettysburg to act as a constable, and was jailed during the town's brief occupation by Confederate forces in June 1863 for the resistance he displayed to Major General Jubal A. Early. On the first day of the Battle of Gettysburg, Burns walked to the scene of the fighting with his old flintlock rifle and requisitioned a more modern gun from a wounded Union soldier. He went on to fight with a number of different units before his wounds forced him off the field, and he sought treatment from Confederate medics after convincing them he was a noncombatant. He died in 1872.

After the Confederate repulse on McPherson Ridge, a lull descended on the field as the opposing forces brought up reinforcements. In the afternoon, Confederate general Richard Ewell's Second Corps launched an assault north of Gettysburg that overwhelmed the thinly held Union line. The defending Eleventh Corps collapsed, which unhinged the entire Union line. Men in blue were soon fleeing into town, closely pursued by their Southern counterparts, flushed with victory.

Among the Union defenders on the first day of battle was a sixty-nine-year-old former constable, John L. Burns. A veteran of the War of 1812, Burns took up his obsolete flintlock rifle and joined the Federal forces defending McPherson Ridge. Despite being wounded three times on July 1, he survived the battle and became a national hero. Burns joined Lincoln during the National Cemetery dedication in November 1863.

LITTLE ROUND TOP, GETTYSBURG, PA
General Lee was unable to build on his initial gains

The initial Confederate success on the first day of battle convinced Lee of the soundness of continuing the struggle. However, by July 2, 1863, most of the Union army was concentrated in a far stronger position than the previous day. Despite the odds, Lee decided to launch a flank attack against the Union left, similar to Jackson's assault at Chancellorsville. Without Jackson at the helm, it took hours to organize the attack.

The attack, made by two divisions of Longstreet's Corps, struck an overextended Union line. Desperate fighting swirled around boulder-strewn Devil's Den and Little Round Top, a key elevation on the Union flank. Just when the rebels appeared poised to take the summit, Federal reinforcements under Colonel Strong Vincent arrived at Little Round Top to save the strategic location. Today, monument-crowned Little Round Top is one of the most popular tourist stops on the battlefield.

DEVIL'S DEN AND LITTLE ROUND TOP, GETTYSBURG, PA
After the three days of fighting that followed Pickett's Charge, bodies covered the battlefield at Gettysburg

DEVIL'S DEN

Devil's Den, a jumbled cluster of immense boulders at the base of Little Round Top, became a Southern citadel of stone for the remainder of the battle. One of the Southerners killed trying to take Devil's Den was a young man shot in a nearby field. After the battle, the unburied soldier became the subject of a series of images taken by veteran photographer Alexander Gardner. Dissatisfied with the body's original location, Gardner's crew moved the corpse to an alcove within Devil's Den, which was later claimed by Gardner to be a sharpshooter's den.

Unable to crush the Union flanks on July 2, Lee opted to storm the Union center on July 3. The attack, known as "Pickett's Charge," was a spectacular failure that only added to the death toll. The charge is named after Major General George Pickett, one of three Confederate generals who led the charge under its commander, Lieutenant General James Longstreet. In an attempt to weaken the Union defenses, the infantry assault was preceded by a heavy artillery bombardment, but this had little effect. Nine infantry brigades of around 12,500 Confederate soldiers then advanced toward the Union lines

ABOVE: In the months following the battle, Devil's Den became a popular tourist destination.

under heavy fire. Protected by a low stone wall, the Union men forced back their attackers with over 50 percent casualties. At the end of the three-day contest, the Gettysburg battlefield was strewn with the dead and dying. More than 50,000 men fell at Gettysburg—nearly one out of every three soldiers who participated in the epic battle.

GENERAL LEE'S HEADQUARTERS, GETTYSBURG, PA
Where Robert E. Lee planned the battle that ultimately decided the fate of the Confederacy

After the battle, images of Gettysburg were extremely marketable. To meet public demand, photographers flocked to Gettysburg to produce images of key battlefield landmarks. Although Alexander Gardner and others arrived on the battlefield earlier, Mathew Brady was the first photographer to capture the Widow Thompson House, which was utilized by Lee as his headquarters during the battle. The house, originally built in 1834, provided an ideal location for Lee, as it was situated at the center and rear of his battle lines. It was also on the same road used by his advancing soldiers.

GENERAL GEORGE PICKETT

General George Pickett came from one of Virginia's prominent families. During the Mexican-American War, Pickett became famous for carrying the American flag over the walls at Chapultepec. Pickett began the Civil War as a colonel, and was promoted to brigadier general in January 1862. He led his brigade into combat for the first time during the Peninsula Campaign, where he was severely wounded. Pickett did not see serious combat again until the third day at Gettysburg when his division participated in the charge that would forever be associated with his name. Following Gettysburg, he fought without distinction at New Berne and Petersburg. He was relieved of duty following the disastrous rout of his command at Five Forks; however, in the chaos that ensued during the retreat to Appomattox, he was not told of his dismissal.

At the time of the battle, the house was probably arranged over two floors. The eastern side of the house was occupied by Lee and his staff, while the widow Mary Thompson lived in the western side. During the battle, Mrs. Thompson and her daughter-in-law and two small children probably sheltered in the cellar beneath the house. The thick stone walls offered both the family and the general protection from stray artillery shells—another reason for Lee to locate his headquarters here.

ABOVE: In 1922 the house was opened to the public as the Lee Museum by C. F. Daley, who began a collection of items found on the battlefield by visiting veterans. The house has continued to act as a museum ever since. Today, as the Lee's Headquarters Museum, it is one of the oldest museums in Gettysburg.

VICKSBURG, MS

Occupying an important position high above the Mississippi, Vicksburg was regarded by Lincoln as the key to the end of the Civil War

BELOW: The USS *Cairo* was one of the unique, flat-bottomed ironclad gunboats built by the Union navy to operate on interior waterways. It was sunk by underwater torpedoes in December 1862, but a century later was raised from the river and is now an exhibit at Vicksburg National Military Park.

BELOW RIGHT: On April 16, 1863, Union gunboats under Admiral Porter's command slipped downstream past Vicksburg to support Grant's final campaign against the river citadel.

At the very moment that the fighting at Gettysburg was beginning, the brutal forty-seven-day siege of Vicksburg was drawing to a close. Vicksburg, located on bluffs high above the Mississippi River, was the key to this vital waterway. In happier times, side-wheelers could be seen steaming along the river from the cupola of the county courthouse (pictured at left). If the Confederates lost control of the Mississippi River, their infant nation would be torn in half. Lincoln, a Kentuckian by birth and an Illinoisan by adoption, grew up traveling on the flatboats that traversed the Mississippi and its tributaries. He too recognized the enormous strategic importance of Vicksburg. In November 1861, Lincoln remarked to a group of Union officers, "Vicksburg is the key. The war can never be brought to a close until that key is in our pocket."

ADMIRAL DAVID DIXON PORTER

Admiral David Dixon Porter was born into one of the most famous navy families in American history. His grandfather served as a captain during the American Revolution and his father became a commodore during the War of 1812. Porter's adopted brother David Glasgow Farragut would also become a celebrated navy commander during the Civil War. As commander of the Federal Mississippi Squadron, he worked closely with army commanders Ulysses S. Grant and William T. Sherman to secure rivers for the Union. Although his 1864 Red River command was unsuccessful, he was soon transferred east to command the North Atlantic Blockading Squadron. During the assault on Fort Fisher in January 1865, he commanded the largest American fleet ever assembled to that date. After the war, Porter became the superintendent of the U.S. Naval Academy. He died in 1891.

GRANT'S LODGING AT VICKSBURG, MS

General Grant's campaign to take the city took patience and determination

GENERAL ULYSSES S. GRANT

General Ulysses S. Grant was a West Point graduate who served with distinction in the Mexican-American War. Following the conflict, he was assigned to remote outposts in California. Separated from his family and serving under a difficult superior, Grant resigned from the army in 1854 under a cloud of suspicion. When the Civil War erupted, he petitioned for a commission, and quickly rose to the rank of brigadier general; he achieved his first major successes at Forts Henry and Donelson in western Tennessee. In the years that followed, Grant would prove himself one of the Union's ablest commanders. After bold victories at Vicksburg and Chattanooga, President Lincoln promoted Grant to lieutenant general and gave him command of all the Union armies. As overall army commander, he insisted on a coordinated strategy against the Confederate armies in the east and west. Within a year of taking command, Grant forced the surrender of the South's greatest army at Appomattox. His accomplishments on the battlefield led to his election as president in 1868 and again in 1872.

The job of taking Vicksburg fell on the stooped shoulders of Union general Ulysses S. Grant. Grant, a failure in both the peacetime army and private life, had gained a reputation as a pugnacious fighter. Despite being surprised at Shiloh, he had risen to command the principal Union army in the west. Given the enormous obstacles facing the Federal army, perhaps no other Union general was better suited for the daunting task of taking Vicksburg.

For seven months, Grant was consumed with attempts to take the city. In late 1862, he began an unsuccessful overland campaign against Vicksburg. Grant was forced to retreat, and his chief lieutenant, General William T. Sherman, was repulsed at Chickasaw Bayou. Undaunted, Grant determined to renew the contest in the spring. His untiring efforts would eventually meet with success, and he stayed in this house in occupied Vicksburg.

CAPTURED CANNON AT VICKSBURG, MS

Following a forty-seven-day siege, Confederate forces finally surrendered

Grant had to devise a way to come to grips with the army defending Vicksburg. In late April 1863, Grant's army embarked on one of the most brilliant campaigns of the war. He ordered his men to march down the west bank of the Mississippi and cross the great river south of Vicksburg. In a series of running battles, Grant captured the state capital at Jackson and forced the Confederates back into the defenses of Vicksburg.

Unable to take the Southern bastion by storm, Grant settled down for a siege. For the Confederates defending the city, Vicksburg was a death trap. Unable to escape, they slowly starved. On July 4, 1863, after the siege, the rebels capitulated, surrendering enormous amounts of small arms and cannons. Today it is hard to imagine the hundreds of captured ordnance wagons that once sat in the shadow of Vicksburg's churches.

LEFT: One of the methods Grant explored to subdue Vicksburg was a canal across De Soto Point opposite Vicksburg. The canal, if successful, would have allowed Mississippi River traffic to bypass Vicksburg completely. A small portion of the canal is protected today by the National Park Service.

EAST BATTERY, CHARLESTON, SC

General Beauregard and his men fought hard to repel the Union navy, but many buildings suffered heavy damage

To the east of Vicksburg, Union forces were equally determined to take Charleston, a key Southern port and symbol of Confederate resistance. In April 1863, a fleet of Yankee ironclad warships under the command of Rear

Admiral Samuel Du Pont attempted to storm past Fort Sumter and break into Charleston Harbor. However, the rebel defenders, ably led by General P. G. T. Beauregard, easily repulsed the dreaded iron monsters, sinking one of them.

Many of the houses on East Battery fell victim to Union shelling, including the burned-out Daniel Heyward House seen here at right. Shortly after the photograph was taken, the structure crumbled during the Union occupation.

THE FORTIFICATIONS OF CHARLESTON

The fortifications of Charleston included substantial gun emplacements along the battery and in White Point Garden, both prominent landmarks on the Charleston peninsula. In the foreground is a ten-inch Columbiad smoothbore cannon, abandoned by the Confederates when they evacuated Charleston in February 1865. The background of the image features the harbor light, a large lantern located at the center of White Point Garden.

RIGHT: The remains of a Blakely gun destroyed by Confederates before their evacuation of Charleston.

Frustrated in their attempt to break into the harbor, the Northerners launched a combined army-navy expedition against Morris Island in July 1863. The ambitious assault left nearly the entire island in Union hands, except for the northern tip of the island, which was guarded by Batteries Wagner and Gregg. The two bastions, located just yards from Fort Sumter, held out until September. Once they fell, Fort Sumter and Charleston itself were at the mercy of the Yankee cannons.

Quincy Gilmore, the hero of Fort Pulaski, was in command of the Union cannoneers on Morris Island. Gilmore was convinced he could destroy Sumter with a barrage launched from the island. Even before the fall of Batteries Wagner and Gregg, Gilmore began a sustained bombardment of Sumter. The Confederates countered—not just with guns but also with palmetto logs used to make crude repairs to the battered fort.

Makeshift repairs could not compensate for the damage wreaked by the constant pounding of the heavy guns. The walls were pulverized into rubble, transforming the brick citadel into a powerful earthwork. Although most of the fort's cannons were dismounted by the sustained bombardment, the rebels continued to maintain a substantial presence at Sumter. On the night of September 8, 1863, the Sumter garrison repulsed a Union storming party intent on capturing the fort.

LEFT: This view of the interior of Fort Sumter taken by a Confederate photographer in 1864 shows the extent of the damage inflicted by the heavy guns.

FORT SUMTER, CHARLESTON, SC
Despite damage caused by Federal guns, Sumter struggled on with makeshift repairs

BATTERY WAGNER

On July 10, 1863, Union forces under the cover of naval artillery attacked Morris Island. The Federals quickly overran most of the island, but were unable to secure the Confederate batteries Wagner and Gregg. The first attempt to take Wagner by assault occurred the next day. The second attempt, on July 18, is best remembered for a charge made by an African American regiment, the Fifty-fourth Massachusetts Volunteer Infantry. Their brave but ultimately unsuccessful attack was immortalized in the 1989 movie *Glory*.

LEFT: A breach in the north wall of the fort was patched with wickerwork gabions to protect the masonry from further damage.

LEFT: A Union shell remains embedded in the wall of Fort Sumter today.

LEE & GORDON'S MILLS, CHICKAMAUGA, GA
General Bragg secured a victory at Chickamauga that looked to reverse Confederate fortunes in Georgia

GENERAL BRAXTON BRAGG

General Braxton Bragg was a diligent student at West Point, graduating fifth in his class. He gained national fame during the Mexican-American War through his exploits as a commander of artillery. He also gained the admiration of a colonel of Mississippi volunteers, Jefferson Davis. At the commencement of the Civil War, Bragg served in senior posts in Pensacola, Florida, and Corinth, Mississippi. In June 1862, he was promoted to command of the Army of Tennessee. His invasion of Kentucky in the fall of 1862 marked the pinnacle of his success as a Confederate commander; following Perryville, his tenure as commander of the South's largest western army was marred by defeat, wasted opportunities, and unexploited victories. Following the humiliating loss of Chattanooga, Davis ordered him to Richmond to serve as his military advisor. He died in Galveston, Texas, in 1876.

The defeats at Vicksburg and Gettysburg cast a pall over the Confederacy. The only hope for restoring Southern fortunes seemed to be a concentration of rebel forces in northern Georgia. On September 19, 1863, Confederate general Braxton Bragg threw his reinforced legions across Chickamauga Creek in Georgia in an effort to crush the Union Army of the Cumberland. One of the few landmarks in the vicinity was Lee & Gordon's Mills, located on the southern extremity of the battlefield.

The fighting on September 19, 1863, was inconclusive. The next day, Bragg resumed his attacks, seeking a weak spot in the Union line. The Confederates eventually found a gap created when the Union commander juggled his forces to plug another gap that didn't exist. The result was a tremendous Southern victory that seemed to reverse the tide of the war. Today much of the battlefield is preserved as part of Chickamauga and Chattanooga National Military Park.

MISSIONARY RIDGE, CHATTANOOGA, TN

Union soldiers waited for reinforcements while under siege by Bragg's forces

After the debacle of Chickamauga, the survivors of the Army of the Cumberland streamed back to their supply base at Chattanooga. The Yankee army, battered and dispirited, was in dire straits. Only Bragg's lackluster pursuit, combined with

Union general George H. Thomas's heroic stand on Snodgrass Hill, prevented the Chickamauga defeat from becoming a disaster. On September 23, 1863, Bragg lay siege to Chattanooga by taking control of Missionary Ridge.

BELOW: A Mathew Brady photograph of Missionary Ridge taken from a fortification at Orchard Knob. At the base of the ridge were lines of Confederate rifle pits that would be assaulted head-on by Major General George H. Thomas once the Union assembled its forces in November.

CHATTANOOGA

Chattanooga was a railroad town of strategic significance to both the Union and Confederacy. The railroads that radiated out of the city connected eastern Tennessee with the Deep South and Virginia. After its occupation by Union forces in September 1863, Chattanooga became an armed camp. During the siege of the town that followed Chickamauga, the encircled Federal forces were nearly starved out. Grant's victory at Chattanooga in November ensured that the town would become a base of operations against Atlanta in 1864.

RIGHT: The desolate slopes of Missionary Ridge, up which Confederate troops scrambled in retreat after being forced out of their rifle pits by the overwhelming Union forces led by General Thomas.

For two months, the Army of the Cumberland sat in besieged Chattanooga, surviving on reduced rations and awaiting succor from Union armies under Generals Grant and Hooker. Grant was given overall command of the forces around Chattanooga, with the understanding that his immediate objective was the defeat of Bragg. In late October 1863, he opened the "cracker line" to supply the Army of the Cumberland, and on November 24 he launched his attack against Bragg.

91

ABOVE: Four men from Company B, Seventy-eighth Pennsylvania Infantry Regiment.

BELOW: An unidentified Union cavalry officer poses for photographers Royan and James Linn. In late 1863, after the Battles of Lookout Mountain and Missionary Ridge, the pair set up a studio near Point Lookout.

LOOKOUT MOUNTAIN, TN

Union forces won against Bragg's weak defenses after a day of fighting on the mountain

Grant's offensive began with an assault led by Hooker against Lookout Mountain, an 1,100-foot precipice that anchored Bragg's left flank. Despite the natural advantages the forbidding terrain offered to the defense, Bragg left the mountain sparsely guarded, which allowed the Union to secure an easy victory. Perhaps because of the fog that day, the fighting on Lookout Mountain was referred to by a Union general as "the Battle Above the Clouds."

The next day, Grant sent Sherman against Bragg's right flank, hoping that Sherman could force the evacuation of Missionary Ridge. However, Sherman was stalled by Confederate general Patrick Cleburne's skillful defense of Tunnel Hill. It then fell upon the Army of the Cumberland to attack Missionary Ridge in an assault that routed the rebels in a manner reminiscent of the Union rout at Chickamauga two months before.

ABOVE: Looking down on Chattanooga from Lookout Mountain. Although seemingly a strong position to defend, Confederate artillerymen were unable to depress their guns enough to support their brigades at the strategically important "bench" below the main ridge.

GENERAL JOSEPH HOOKER

Union general Joseph Hooker, whose rapid rise to military prominence was cut short by defeat at Chancellorsville in May, hoped to resuscitate his moribund career at Chattanooga. He performed well at Lookout Mountain in November, earning a brevet to major general in the regular army. However, his proclivity for pulling political strings did not endear him with Sherman, and he was eventually passed over for promotion.

ABOVE: Today, Point Lookout and Umbrella Rock (not pictured) are hardly changed from their Civil War appearance, although access is restricted.

RAPIDAN RIVER, VA
The Battle of the Wilderness was bloody and inconclusive, but gave a boost to the Army of the Potomac

LEFT, ABOVE, AND RIGHT: Germanna Ford on the Rapidan River. Union troops under General Grant crossed here on May 4, 1864. Grant's plan was to move quickly and place his forces between General Lee and the city of Richmond. The long caravan of supply wagons is visible stretching into the distance in both historic photos.

BELOW: Confederate entrenchments on the Wilderness battlefield near the McCool house. A makeshift sign commemorates fallen soldiers.

Due in large measure to his victory at Chattanooga, Grant was brought east in March 1864 to take command of all the Union armies. Rather than sit behind a desk in Washington, Grant chose to make his headquarters with the ill-fated Army of the Potomac. In May, he led that army southward, across the Rapidan River at Germanna Ford and into the Wilderness, where the Confederate army of Robert E. Lee was waiting.

The two-day Battle of the Wilderness pitted more than 160,000 soldiers in gray and blue against one another in one of the bloodiest struggles of the Civil War. Fought in the thickets and secondary-growth forest of Spotsylvania County, the battle was a series of clashes for control of the few roads in the vicinity. The result was a tactical draw, but Grant's refusal to retreat back across the Rapidan gave him a moral victory.

ABOVE: The Wilderness Tavern located near the intersection of the Orange Turnpike and Germanna Plank Road. The tavern site served as a field hospital during Chancellorsville and the Wilderness.

SPOTSYLVANIA COURT HOUSE, VA

Tactically significant, this crossroads town saw two weeks of combat, including a twenty-three-hour stretch of nonstop fighting

After the Battle of the Wilderness, the armies raced for the crossroads town of Spotsylvania, located on the main road to Richmond. Lee won the race, but by the slimmest of margins. His dismounted cavalry held off the Union army just long enough for the Confederate infantry to arrive. At the time of the battle, Spotsylvania itself was little more than a cluster of buildings, along with the courthouse shown in the above image.

HARRIS FARM

The struggle for the Harris Farm, fought in the late afternoon of May 19, 1864, occurred at the tail end of the Battle of Spotsylvania. The short but bloody fight would likely have been forgotten by most historians except for a series of extraordinary photographs taken by Timothy O'Sullivan. O'Sullivan, coincidentally traveling near the site of the unexpected battle, was able to record the burial of Confederate dead the following day.

BELOW: The Beverly house, headquarters of Major General Gouverneur K. Warren of the Union Fifth Corps.

ABOVE: The battering sustained by the courthouse during the Civil War necessitated major repairs in 1870. By 1900 the building was declared unsafe; subsequently, a new, enlarged building of similar design was constructed on the site, using cream bricks instead of red.

For two weeks, the opposing armies parried and thrust on the outskirts of Spotsylvania. The worst day was May 12, 1864, when the Union Second Corps managed to break the Southern line at what came to be called the "Bloody Angle." For twenty-three straight hours, the two sides struggled against one another in the longest period of sustained combat of the war. Today, more than 1,300 acres of the Spotsylvania battlefield are protected within the national park system.

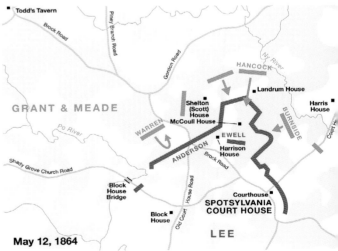

Todd's Tavern

Brock Road

Piney Branch Road

Gordon Road

Ny River

HANCOCK

GRANT & MEADE

Shelton (Scott) House

McCoull House

Landrum House

Harris House

BURNSIDE

WARREN

Po River

ANDERSON

EWELL

Harrison House

Brock Road

Court Ho

Shady Grove Church Road

Block House Bridge

Old Court House Road

Courthouse

SPOTSYLVANIA COURT HOUSE

Block House

LEE

May 12, 1864

MASSAPONAX CHURCH, SPOTSYLVANIA, VA

After some of the worst fighting of the war, the armies moved south and General Grant established a temporary base at this church

That evening, Lee withdrew from the Bloody Angle, taking up a shorter line just south of the scene of the fight on May 12, 1864. The carnage of the Bloody Angle left many a combatant nearly speechless. According to a Massachusetts soldier, "I cannot begin to tell you the horrors I have seen . . . the rebels are piled up in heaps three or four deep and the pit is filled with them piled up dead and wounded."

The fighting at Spotsylvania continued, but the worst was over. On May 20–21, 1864, after the Battle of Harris Farm, the crippled armies abandoned their lines outside the town and began moving south toward Richmond. During the march, Grant's headquarters were briefly located on borrowed pews outside Massaponax Church. The church retains its wartime appearance today.

LEFT: Two days after recording the dead of Harris Farm, Timothy O'Sullivan captured the Union high command sitting on pews taken outside Massaponax Church. In this image, the overall commander of the Union armies, Ulysses S. Grant, can be seen looking over the shoulder of the seated George Meade, commander of the Army of the Potomac. In the background, wagons emblazed with the Maltese cross emblem of the Fifth Corps can be seen traveling south toward the North Anna River.

BLANDFORD CHURCH, PETERSBURG, VA

The transportation hub of Petersburg became Grant's target in his bid to secure victory for the Union in Virginia

THE BATTLE OF NORTH ANNA

The Battle of North Anna was one of the great "ifs" of the Civil War. Grant rashly divided his army into three parts, separated by the North Anna River (above). By doing so, he was playing into Lee's hands. Lee intended to throw the bulk of his army against one of Grant's isolated wings. However, illness prevented Lee from leading the attack in person, and the caution of Lee's subordinates enabled Grant to slip out of the trap.

BELOW: A redoubt near the Dunn house on the outer line of Confederate fortifications that were captured June 14, 1864, by General William F. Smith.

Throughout May and early June 1864, Lee's Army of Northern Virginia would continue to parry Grant's attempts to leapfrog between the Confederate army and Richmond. The armies clashed at North Anna, Totopotomoy Creek, and Cold Harbor, in the process lengthening already unprecedented casualty lists. Finally, Grant concluded that victory lay not in front of Richmond but to the south, at the vital railroad center of Petersburg.

On the night of June 12, 1864, Grant moved to occupy Petersburg. For once, he got the jump on Lee, who had not anticipated a Union move toward Petersburg. However, fierce resistance by General P. G. T. Beauregard prevented Grant from taking the city. The roar of the guns could be heard at Petersburg's Blandford Church, first photographed by Timothy O'Sullivan. The church is today preserved as a war memorial, with stained-glass windows depicting the short life of the Confederacy.

GRANT'S HEADQUARTERS, CITY POINT, VA
During the siege of Petersburg, Grant and his men lived in huts overlooking the James and Appomattox Rivers

COLLIS'S ZOUAVES

The 114th Pennsylvania, also known as Collis's Zouaves after its first commander, was recruited in the summer of 1862. The regiment fought in some of the most desperate battles of the war, including Chancellorsville, Gettysburg, and Petersburg. In March 1864, the regiment and its band were detailed to the headquarters of the Army of the Potomac to serve as headquarters guard and provide music for army commander George Meade.

BELOW: Grant's winter quarters at City Point were so long-lived that a semipermanent infrastructure was established, including telegraph lines and this post office.

The failure to take Petersburg was a major blow to Grant's hopes to end the war in 1864. The fighting that raged just outside the city on June 15–18 held the promise of victory, but both the Union commanders and their troops were lacking the spirit and élan they displayed at the beginning of the campaign. Recognizing that his battered army was not in any condition to launch an attack against earthworks, Grant settled in for a siege.

Grant made his headquarters at City Point, on the heights over the confluence of the James and Appomattox Rivers. Here, alongside Appomattox Manor, his aides and staff officers built log huts and bivouacked until April 1865. Of the multitude of huts, only Grant's survived. After the war, it was taken to Philadelphia, where it rested for more than a century. It was eventually returned to City Point.

BELOW: The "Dictator" was a thirteen-inch mortar used by Union forces in the siege of Petersburg. The mortar could fire a 225-pound exploding shell up to two miles and took fourteen pounds of black power. It was mounted on the flatbed of a railroad car, which allowed it to vary the direction of bombardment.

FORT SEDGWICK, PETERSBURG, VA

The fortified earthworks outside Petersburg during the siege provided a miserable existence for soldiers on both sides

The brutal siege of Petersburg would consume nearly ten months and many lives. For America, the miles of dank and dirty ditches, connecting scores of equally dismal forts, were a precursor to the miserable trenches on the western front during World War I. Fort Sedgwick's close proximity to Fort Mahone made service in the bastion a particularly onerous ordeal.

The men who garrisoned Fort Sedgwick referred to their stronghold as "Fort Hell." Their counterparts in gray dubbed Fort Mahone "Fort Damnation." The duel between the earthen citadels symbolized the entire siege—the two sides could do little to one another except add to the misery and body count. Today, no traces of Fort Sedgwick survive; the site has been leveled for parking lots and a postwar railroad underpass, though the name survives in a nearby street name.

LEFT: A gabioned parapet at Sedgwick. During the Civil War, men displaced earth, removed timber for building material, and erected large structures for massive engineering projects, all of which altered familiar terrain. Fort Sedgwick, designed by Major Washington Roebling, was a notable example of defenses carved out of the earth.

RESACA BATTLEFIELD, GA
Attempts by the Union to cut Confederate supply lines forced Johnston's forces into retreat

As the armies in the East began their bloody promenade from the Rapidan to Richmond, the principal antagonists in Georgia were engaged in a life-and-death struggle in northwestern Georgia. In early May 1864, General Sherman launched his spring campaign, with Atlanta as its objective. After ten days of skirmishing and maneuvering, the armies wound up at Resaca, a strategic railroad town next to the Oostanaula River.

Sherman's goal was to cut the supply line of his Confederate counterpart, General Joseph Johnston, by burning the railroad bridge seen in the wartime photograph. His first attempt, on May 9, 1864, failed because of an overcautious commander. His second try, on May 14–15, resulted in a stalemate, as neither side was able to land a knockout blow. On the evening of May 15, Johnston retreated across the Oostanaula, at the site of the present-day railroad bridge.

BELOW: Confederate earthworks overlooking the battlefield at Resaca in 1864. From their position, Johnston and his men were able to withstand attacks from Sherman's men, but when Union forces began to threaten from the rear, the rebels were forced to retreat south. Nature has reclaimed the site today.

GENERAL WILLIAM T. SHERMAN

William Tecumseh Sherman is one of the most misunderstood and controversial generals of the Civil War. His predictions of a long war and concern about heavy casualties cast a shadow over his career early in the war. However, his successful partnership with Grant at Shiloh and during the Vicksburg campaign catapulted him to the high command. When Grant was sent east to command all the Union armies, he placed Sherman in overall command of the three major western armies. Sherman led his men to victory at Atlanta, launched his legendary March to the Sea in the fall of 1864, and then headed northward through the Carolinas. He accepted the surrender of the second-largest Confederate army in late April 1865.

RIGHT: A map of Resaca and vicinity produced by the Western and Atlantic Railroad Company shows entrenchments, roads, railroads, towns, drainage, and relief by hachures.

MATTHEWS, NORTHRUP & CO., ART-PRINTING WORKS, BUFFALO, N.Y.

KENNESAW MOUNTAIN BATTLEFIELD, GA

A bold assault here by General Sherman's men initially proved successful but was later repulsed

Sherman followed Johnston southward, nipping at his heels along the way. The two erstwhile adversaries fought a series of sharp but indecisive battles between the Oostanaula and Etowah Rivers. On June 27, 1864, Sherman abandoned

his previously successful strategy of outflanking his opponent in favor of a frontal assault. Believing that Johnston's Kennesaw Mountain line was overextended, Sherman attacked the rebels who were dug in along Pigeon Hill and Cheatham Hill.

ABOVE AND TOP RIGHT: The battlefield at Kennesaw. Sherman's army consisted of 100,000 men, 254 guns, and 35,000 horses; Johnston had 63,000 men and 187 guns under his command. Over 67,000 soldiers were killed, wounded, or captured during the campaign. Matching trees in the historic photos show that they were taken from similar positions.

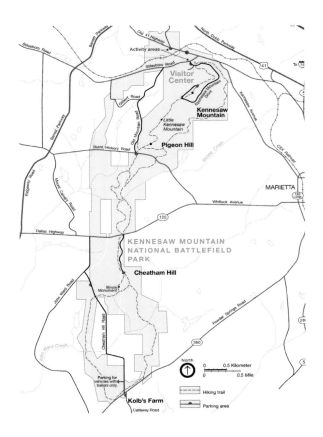

Sherman's men were simply not up to this daunting task, although they did manage to penetrate the Confederate line in several places. At Pigeon Hill in particular, the bluecoats secured the first line of rebel trenches and seemed intent on exploiting their brief victory. The fight soon degenerated into a hand-to-hand brawl that cost more than 4,000 lives. Today, more than 2,800 acres of the Kennesaw Mountain battlefield are protected from development.

RIGHT: The National Battlefield Park at Kennesaw Mountain. The main site is located at Cheatham Hill (then commonly known as the Dead Angle), where there is a visitor center. There are also 17.3 miles of interpretive walking trails featuring historic earthworks, cannon emplacements, and various interpretive signs. Three monuments represent the states that fought here.

FORTS AROUND ATLANTA, GA
As the Union closed in on Atlanta, Johnston's troops dug in, but he was replaced by John B. Hood, who went on the offensive

Smarting from his repulse at Kennesaw Mountain, Sherman returned to the flanking maneuvers that had proven so successful over the past seven weeks. Johnston was again forced to retreat, eventually falling back across the Chattahoochee River—the last water barrier between the Union forces and Atlanta. Johnston dug in, constructing a series of earthen forts around the city. However, the forts were destined to be defended by another man. On July 17, 1864, President Davis replaced the cautious Johnston with General John B. Hood. Hood was not the type of commander who would wait to be outflanked by Sherman's host. He was determined to seize the initiative and throw the Union troops back from Atlanta. Three days after taking the helm, Hood sallied forth from his earthworks and threw his army against an isolated segment of the Federal army. Residential housing now sits where the earthworks once stood.

LEFT: An unidentified rebel fort in front of Atlanta. Civil War historians have yet to pinpoint its exact location.

BELOW: A Union army picket post near Atlanta in November 1864. Pickets provided advance outposts or guards for a large force. It was a hazardous job, and as pickets were the first to feel any major enemy movements, they were often the first to be killed, wounded, or captured. Picket duty, by regulation, was rotated regularly in a regiment.

ABOVE: Another George Barnard photo from 1864. The original caption reads: "The view from a Confederate fort, east of Peachtree Street, looking east."

BELOW: Today, much of the city's most important architecture can be found on Peachtree Street, which is the route for numerous annual parades.

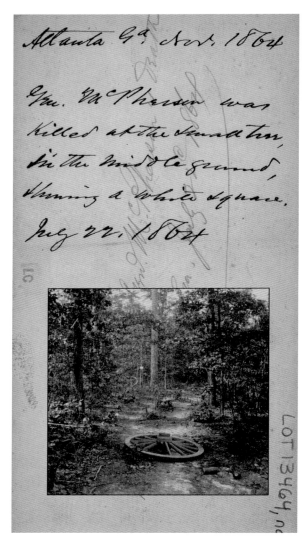

Atlanta Ga. Nov. 1864

Gen. McPherson was killed at the Small tree, in the middle ground, showing a white square. July 22. 1864

McPHERSON DEATH SITE, ATLANTA, GA

Fighting raged around Atlanta as Union forces advanced, but a brave general was lost

The cost of the fighting around Atlanta was heavy on both sides. Hood's offensive at Peachtree Creek was followed by other, equally bloody battles that did little more than weaken the Confederate army's ability to hold its lines around Atlanta. One of the casualties of these early battles was General James McPherson, who was killed when he accidentally rode into Confederate lines. A Union photographer later captured the scene of McPherson's death.

From the middle of July through the end of August 1864, Atlanta joined the long list of Southern cities besieged by invaders from the North. Hood's valiant but ill-fated attempts to reverse the Union tide only accelerated the inevitable. The fighting at Atlanta, Ezra Church, and Utoy Creek merely tightened Sherman's stranglehold on the city. Today an upright cannon (right) marks the spot where McPherson was killed during the Battle of Atlanta.

ABOVE LEFT: General McPherson was killed at the small tree in the middle ground, showing a white square, on July 22, 1864; the photo was taken in November 1864. Civil War photographers often added props—such as the cart wheel and the shell cases—to make photos more dramatic.

ABOVE: The original image together with the description of this historic event written on the reverse by photographer George Barnard.

GENERAL JAMES B. McPHERSON

General James B. McPherson was a career army officer who served with distinction under both Grant and Sherman. He graduated first in the same West Point class that produced future Civil War generals Philip Sheridan and John B. Hood. McPherson served as Grant's chief engineer during the Fort Henry, Donelson, and Shiloh campaigns. At Champion Hill, he led the Union Seventeenth Corps to victory. After Sherman's promotion to command the western armies, McPherson assumed command of the Army of the Tennessee. McPherson's army has been described as Sherman's "whiplash" during the Atlanta campaign, serving as the principal weapon to outflank the Confederate army defending Georgia. On July 22, in the wake of a surprise counterattack by Hood, McPherson rode forward to investigate the situation and was killed.

OCCUPATION OF ATLANTA, GA

With Hood's men in retreat, Sherman's troops marched into a devastated city

By the end of August 1864, an impasse had been reached. Hood's aggressive tactics had cost him more than 11,000 men, leaving his Army of Tennessee demoralized and dispirited. On August 25, Sherman struck southwest of Atlanta, severing the Macon and Western Railroad, Hood's last remaining supply line. After a final, foiled attempt to regain the railroad at Jonesboro, Hood was forced to give up Atlanta. On the night of September 1, 1864, his battered army evacuated.

LEFT AND TOP: The large photograph shows the railroad depot and its surroundings, along with loaded carts and wagons. In the smaller image, soldiers of the First Michigan Engineers and Mechanics Regiment destroy railroad tracks in Atlanta, with the ruins of the car shed visible on the right of the photo.

ABOVE: The office of the *Daily Intelligencer* newspaper near the railroad depot, shortly after the surrender of Atlanta.

Sherman's triumphant armies entered Atlanta the next day. He telegraphed Washington: "Atlanta is ours, and fairly won." Prior to Atlanta, Northerners—numbed by the endless casualty lists of the past summer—despaired for victory. Lincoln, unable to demonstrate success, was convinced he would lose the November presidential election. The fall of Atlanta transformed Northern opinion toward the war. The end was finally within sight.

ABOVE: In the modern photo, the building below the whale mural on the right is the freight depot, built in 1867. The current railroad tracks still run on the other side of the depot, through the basement of the parking garage on which the whale mural is painted.

ABOVE: The Union Depot was an Atlanta landmark. Built by architect Edward Vincent in 1853, it served several railroads. During the Confederate evacuation, the depot was the scene of chaos as people tried to get belongings on the last train out. In November 1864, the depot was destroyed by Sherman's army as it prepared to leave Atlanta to begin the March to the Sea.

RIGHT: When the triumphant Federals entered the city, they witnessed scenes of devastation such as this mill, which was destroyed when a nearby ordnance train exploded, leaving only the bogies of the freight cars behind.

ALLATOONA PASS, GA

Hood targeted Sherman's supply line to the west, but Union soldiers were able to defend their position

In the weeks that followed the capture of Atlanta, Sherman rested his army and plotted his next move. Sherman's victory left him deep in hostile territory, dependent on a lengthy and vulnerable supply line that limited his options. Hood, sensing his opponent's quandary, began moving his army northward to strike the vital Western and Atlantic Railroad. On October 5, 1864, Hood struck the railroad at Allatoona Pass (left).

Unfortunately for Hood, Allatoona Pass was a natural citadel. The Union garrison, outnumbered by the attacking rebels, prepared to make a final stand in the Star Fort overlooking the railroad. The stalwart Union defense of Allatoona Pass would inspire a postwar hymn entitled "Hold the Fort." Of the 5,300 men who fought at Allatoona, over 1,600 were casualties. Today, the Allatoona Pass battlefield (right) is preserved as a park by the U.S. Army Corps of Engineers.

TOP: Soldiers stand on a ridge near Allatoona Pass. As the battle unfolded, Confederate general Samuel T. French issued a summon to surrender "in order to avoid a needless effusion of blood."

TOP RIGHT: Allatoona Pass looking into the railroad cut.

LEFT: Allatoona Pass; a view from the hill looking back down the line, photographed by George Barnard, most likely in 1865.

STATE CAPITOL, NASHVILLE, TN

With victory increasingly unlikely, Hood ordered his weakened force to dig in outside Nashville

THE BATTLE OF FRANKLIN

The Battle of Franklin was one of the most lopsided Union victories of the war. After escaping a potential trap at nearby Spring Hill, General John Schofield's Fourth and Twenty-third Corps dug in along the Harper River at Franklin. Hood unwisely launched a frontal assault against Schofield's formidable works, losing more than 6,000 men, including six generals. Much of the battlefield was lost during the twentieth century, but local preservationists are actively trying to reclaim key parts of the battlefield.

RIGHT: A George Barnard photo looking out from the steps of the Nashville State Capitol Building with covered guns. In late 1863, Barnard accepted a position as the Army of the Cumberland's head of photography. While stationed in Nashville, he took pictures of the landscape and fortifications that would gain significance in late 1864.

FAR RIGHT: The rail yard of the Nashville, Chattanooga, and St. Louis Railway with the capitol in the background. The army built the castellated structure as a warehouse for food, clothing, and ammunition.

In November 1864, an incident unusual in modern warfare occurred. The armies of Hood and Sherman turned their backs to one another, with Hood marching northward to Nashville and Sherman marching southeast to Savannah. While Sherman's campaign was crowned with success, Hood's movement into Tennessee was plagued with missed opportunities and defeat. On November 30, he suffered a bloody repulse at Franklin, losing a full quarter of his army. Hood pursued the Union army northward to the gates of Nashville, arriving on December 2. Fortunately for the Union cause, the methodical Major General George H. Thomas had been granted the time he needed to fortify the city, making it nearly impervious to assault. Hood ordered his decimated and demoralized army to dig in outside Nashville. Even today, it is difficult to understand what Hood hoped to accomplish by placing his ill-clad men at the mercy of such a formidable foe.

FORT NEGLEY, NASHVILLE, TN

General Thomas took his time before dealing the final blow to the Confederate forces outside Nashville

While the Confederates shivered in their lines outside Nashville, General George H. Thomas was slowly preparing to lift Hood's quasi siege of the city. Too slowly, in the eyes of his overall commander, Ulysses S. Grant. Impatient with Thomas's sluggish performance, Grant was on the verge of replacing Thomas when the Army of the Cumberland finally ventured from its fortified lines. Shown here is the casemate of Fort Negley, one of the strongest points in the Union line.

The Union attack quickly forced the gray line to fall back. Late in the afternoon of December 16, 1864, blue cavalrymen succeeded in infiltrating the Confederate rear, making the Southern line untenable. Attacked in the flank and rear, the rebel army collapsed, its shattered remnants streaming southward in disarray. Thomas's victory at Nashville crushed once and for all Confederate hopes for independence. Other than Fort Negley, little remains of this historic battlefield today.

ABOVE RIGHT: Looking northeast from Fort Negley, the largest inland fort built during the Civil War. Construction was overseen by Captain James St. Clair Morton, and it used 62,500 cubic feet of stone and 18,000 cubic feet of earth. The fort was named for Union army commander James S. Negley.

FORT FISHER, NC

Guarding the valuable port of Wilmington, Confederate forces withstood attacks until January 1865

While the Union army was busy securing final victory on land, the Union navy was equally active winning the war at sea. The navy's target was the port of Wilmington, North Carolina— the South's only remaining outlet to the outside world. The port was guarded by Fort Fisher, an enormous earthen fortification armed with forty-seven heavy-caliber cannons. The fort was referred to as the "Gibraltar of the Confederacy."

In December 1864, a joint army-navy expedition led by the incompetent General Ben Butler ended in embarrassment for the Union. The fleet assembled for the expedition was photographed before its departure from Hampton Road (right) by Timothy O'Sullivan. Despite the setback, the Union troops regrouped and, under a new commander, launched a second attack in mid-January. After cutting the fort off from the mainland, Union forces launched two separate assaults and eventually breached the fort. Following a hand-to-hand struggle, more than 2,000 Confederates surrendered. Today Fort Fisher is a state historic site.

BELOW: Colonel William Lamb spent two years building up the defenses at Fort Fisher. Atop the parapet he constructed fifteen traverses, which protected the guns from flanking fire.

ABOVE: Union soldiers pose with a shattered Confederate gun captured after the fort was finally overrun in January 1865.

BELOW: Colonel Lamb also oversaw the construction of a land-faced earthen wall that was nearly half a mile long, thirty feet high, and twenty-five feet thick. A wooden palisade impeded the Union infantry, while the land in front of the walls was rigged with electrically triggered land mines. Today the earthworks are preserved as part of Fort Fisher State Historic Park.

STATE CAPITOL, COLUMBIA, SC

As Sherman's men marched into Columbia, the city was ablaze; the capitol was among the buildings that remained

WRECKING RAILROADS

The original 1865 caption to these stereotype images reads: "On the march to the sea Sherman's army burned the bridges and destroyed the railroads as they went. This view [above] gives a view of the destruction of the W. & A. R. R. The rails are first torn up, then the wooden toes are pried out and piled in heaps and burned; the iron rails are laid across the burning ties, and soon get hot enough on the middle so the weight of the ends bend the rail up, as here shown. Of course when they get cold they are simply good as 'old iron.'"

While Hood and Thomas were battling in the middle of Tennessee, the rest of Sherman's army, 62,000 strong, was heading toward the sea. Sherman encountered only limited resistance during the 250-mile march through the heart of the Confederacy. His men destroyed anything that could be of value to the Southern forces. It was said that Sherman's progress could be measured by the smoke of blazing houses. On December 21, 1864, Sherman captured Savannah after an eleven-day siege.

In January 1865, Sherman left Savannah, determined to repeat his march in the Carolinas. Although slowed by bad weather, Sherman's army could not be stopped. On February 17, his men marched into the South Carolina capital of Columbia. By the time they entered Columbia, part of the city was already ablaze with a fire that destroyed half its buildings. Among the structures gutted in the fire was the state capitol. Today six bronze stars indicate where the building was hit by Union cannon fire.

CHARLESTON, SC
The Confederates were forced to abandon this symbolic city

In addition to the capture of Columbia, Sherman's march through South Carolina cut off rebel communications with the port of Charleston. The Confederates had no alternative but to evacuate the city where the war began—a city that had come to symbolize Southern resistance. On February 17, 1865, the same day Columbia fell, Charleston was abandoned without a fight. Among the military ordnance destroyed by the fleeing rebels were enormous Blakely guns imported from England, whose mounting can be seen at the bottom of the archive photograph (left).

The fall of Charleston had an enormous effect on Southern morale. Although the port itself had long been closed by the Union naval blockade, the city had withstood ironclads, armies, and artillery for four long years. Since the July 1863 occupation of Morris Island, Charleston had suffered intermittent bombardment. Confederate president Jefferson Davis remarked that its fall was "extremely bitter" to him. Conversely, the North was overjoyed with the capture of the city where secession began.

ABOVE RIGHT: The view from the roof of the Mills House in 1865, looking up Meeting Street, with the ruins of the Circular Church in the center.

BELOW: The ruins of the Northeastern Railroad depot, photographed by Mathew Brady.

FORT STEDMAN, PETERSBURG, VA

Weakened rebel forces attempted a last-ditch assault here in Virginia, but their early success was short-lived

Back in Virginia, Confederate prospects were not much better. Although Lee still maintained his earthworks around Petersburg, his lines were stretched to the limit. Only the muddy roads prevented Grant from launching an assault that would finally break the thin rebel ranks. Seeing no other way out of his predicament, Lee decided to launch an assault against the Union host, hoping the attack would throw Grant off balance and allow the rebel army to escape Petersburg.

RIGHT: A view of the battlefield at Petersburg taken from a signal tower during the siege.

Lee chose Fort Stedman (left) as the focal point for his onslaught. Due to careful preparation and the element of surprise, the attack was initially successful. But the preponderance of Union forces began to tell. The Confederates were soon forced to abandon the fort and fall back to their lines. Lee's last offensive of the war ended in bleak failure. Today the remains of Fort Stedman (above) are protected within Petersburg National Military Park.

RIGHT: A "bomb-proof" shelter at the Union stronghold of Fort Stedman. It was named for Griffin A. Stedman, a Union colonel who had been killed in the vicinity in August 1864.

LIBBY PRISON, RICHMOND, VA
Union soldiers arrived to find a burning city

Within days of the repulse at Fort Stedman, Grant embarked on his much-anticipated final offensive against Lee. On April 1, 1865, Grant crushed Lee's right flank at the Battle of Five Forks. The next day, Grant moved in for the kill. His attacks on Petersburg broke Lee's line and forced him to evacuate the town, ending the longest siege in American history. Without the vital rail junction of Petersburg, Richmond could no longer be held.

The Confederate government abandoned Richmond on the evening of April 2. Before leaving, they set afire anything of potential value to the approaching Union army. The fire grew out of control, destroying more than 700 buildings in its wake. Within days of Richmond's fall, Northern photographers arrived in the desolate and still-smoldering town. They recorded haunting images, including photos of the nondescript warehouse that had become the infamous Libby Prison.

BURNT DISTRICT

The Union army that Richmond residents had long feared arrived in the city on the morning of April 3. The Federals were quickly thrown into the effort to fight the advancing flames, which had reached within a block of Capitol Square. Although the city was saved, the destruction in the burned-out section was so complete that today the area is still referred to as the "Burnt District."

ABOVE: Castle Thunder, a former tobacco warehouse, was located on Tobacco Row of Cary Street in Richmond. The building was converted into a prison by Confederate forces and was used to house civilians, criminals, Union spies, and others charged with treason.

RIGHT: Libby Prison was another building used by the rebel army to house prisoners of war. It was moved to Chicago in 1889 to serve as a Civil War museum, but was dismantled in 1895 and its pieces sold as souvenirs. A plaque now marks where the building once stood.

APPOMATTOX COURT HOUSE, VA
The Wilmer McLean house was the scene of the surrender of General Lee's forces

WILMER McLEAN

At the outset of the Civil War, Wilmer McLean lived on Yorkshire Farm near the banks of Bull Run. His home came under fire on July 18, 1861, in the days leading up to the Battle of First Manassas. Determined to escape the conflict, he moved his family south to rural Appomattox Court House, where the war found him again in April 1865. The surrender was signed in the front parlor of his house.

ABOVE: The courthouse itself. Today it is a visitor center for the Appomattox Court House National Historical Park.

LEFT: A photograph from Timothy O'Sullivan's 1865 series of the McLean House, formerly the "New" Raine Tavern, with Wilmer McLean's two younger children and two servant girls on the porch.

Freed from having to defend Richmond, General Lee hoped that his smaller, more agile army might still escape Grant's clutches to continue the war elsewhere. However, Lee's ill-fed, ill-clad men were no longer capable of the speedy marches that they once were. On April 9, the wily Lee was finally cornered at Appomattox Court House. That morning, dressed in his finest uniform, he surrendered to Grant in the home of Wilmer McLean.

After Lee's surrender at Appomattox, the remaining Confederate armies began to topple. Within a week, General Joseph Johnston, again in command of the army facing Sherman, approached his erstwhile adversary about terms for surrender. By the end of May, nearly all the remaining Southern armies had capitulated. The final Confederate general to surrender was Cherokee Indian chief Stand Watie, who surrendered his command on June 23.

FORD'S THEATRE, WASHINGTON, D.C.
Tragedy befell the Union when President Lincoln was assassinated during a night out at the theater

Although the defeated South lay in ruins, the first two weeks of April 1865 were a sustained celebration throughout the North. The fall of Petersburg and Richmond, followed by Lee's surrender, meant that the national catastrophe was finally at an end. On the evening of April 14, President Abraham Lincoln, just beginning his second term in office, joined in the revelry by attending a play at Ford's Theatre featuring one of his favorite actresses, Laura Keene.

Lincoln's fatal wounding at Ford's Theatre was the final tragedy of the most tragic war in American history. Shot while sitting in the presidential box by actor John Wilkes Booth, the president succumbed to his wound in a small bedroom across the street from the theater. Upon his death, Secretary of War Edwin M. Stanton was moved to remark, "Now he belongs to the ages." Ford's Theatre is now maintained as a museum by the National Park Service.

TOP LEFT: A poster broadcasting the hunt and reward for the capture of assassin John Wilkes Booth. Booth was on the run for twelve days before he was tracked down in northern Virginia. He refused to give himself up and was shot by a Union soldier.

RIGHT: The presidential box where Abraham Lincoln was assassinated. Today Ford's Theatre provides a comprehensive perspective of Lincoln's life and legacy through exhibits and programs at its theater, museum, and education center.

WASHINGTON, D.C.
Lincoln's death meant the tolerant peace he had imagined became a violent one

In the final months of the war, Lincoln's thoughts were focused on the challenges of reuniting the war-torn nation. In his second inaugural address, Lincoln famously asked his countrymen, North and South, to put aside malice, and urged them to "do all which may achieve and cherish a just and lasting peace." He had similar words for his generals, advising them to go easy on the Confederate armies. Unfortunately, with Lincoln's death, all thoughts of a magnanimous peace evaporated. His successors sought retribution against the rebels as well as Booth's accomplices.

Within weeks of the assassination, the Lincoln conspirators were tried by the military and sentenced to death or imprisonment. Four, including Mary Surratt, were hanged in July 1865. Former Confederate president Jefferson Davis was captured in May and thrown into prison for two years; his predicament generated sympathy for him in both the North and South. Henry Wirz, commandant of the notorious Andersonville Prison in Georgia, was hanged in November 1865, within view of the capitol dome in Washington (left).

TOP RIGHT: Andersonville Prison as seen by John L. Ransom, author and publisher of *Andersonville Diary, Escape and List of the Dead*. Andersonville was officially known as Camp Sumter and was used as a prisoner-of-war camp. Around 13,000 Union prisoners died from disease and malnutrition in this prison in Georgia during the Civil War.

RIGHT: Four Lincoln conspirators—Lewis Paine, David Herold, George Atzerodt, and Mary Surratt—were hanged in the courtyard of the Washington Arsenal on July 7, 1865. Others, like Dr. Samuel Mudd, were given lengthy prison terms for their roles in Booth's actions.

ABOVE: Mary Surratt, along with her three coconspirators, were executed on this site in 1865. Dr. Samuel Mudd, a physician who treated John Wilkes Booth's broken leg as he evaded capture, narrowly avoided the death sentence.

PENNSYLVANIA AVENUE, WASHINGTON, D.C.

The "Grand Review" brought days of celebration to Washington as the new president and the crowds honored Union forces

FORT SUMTER

Fort Sumter, like Charleston, was ultimately evacuated without a fight. On April 14, 1865, four years to the day after he had surrendered the fort, Robert Anderson, now a major general, participated in a special ceremony on the blasted parade ground of the all-but-ruined citadel. Joined by some of the men who served under him during those first early days of the war, Anderson raised over Sumter the same battered flag he had lowered in the spring of 1861.

Mourning gave way to celebration again in late May 1865 when the grizzled veterans of the Union armies marched into Washington for what would forever be remembered as the "Grand Review." On May 24 the victor of Gettysburg, General George Meade, led 80,000 men of the Army of the Potomac down Pennsylvania Avenue to the cheers of spectators. The next day, it was Sherman's Army of the Tennessee and Army of Georgia that marched along Pennsylvania Avenue. The new president, Andrew Johnson, sat in a reviewing stand near the White House. Sherman would later describe the review as "a fitting conclusion to the campaign and the war." Today, a statue of Sherman towers over the site where the reviewing stand was located.

ABOVE: A cavalry division stands at attention on Pennsylvania Avenue during the Grand Review.

HENRY HILL MONUMENT, MANASSAS, VA
Fallen soldiers were also honored on the battlefields where they met their fates, such as this one near Bull Run

Following the Grand Review, veterans of the fighting at Bull Run decided to return to the battlefield to remember their comrades who had died there. Many of them were appalled by the poor condition of the graves. Bleached bones were visible poking out from the ground where they had been shallowly buried. Eventually, the Manassas dead were reinterred in a vault at Arlington National Cemetery.

On June 10, 1865, two stone monuments were dedicated on the Manassas battlefield, commemorating the two battles fought in 1861 and 1862. One monument was placed on Henry House Hill, not far from the family cemetery were Judith Henry was buried. The second monument was placed near the deep cut at Groveton, the scene of heavy fighting in August 1862. Today both monuments are protected by the National Park Service; pictured here is the monument on Henry House Hill.

RIGHT: The dedication of the monument at Groveton.

1913 REUNION AT THE BLOODY ANGLE, GETTYSBURG, PA

Veterans and their families continued to meet for many years to share their Civil War experiences

In the years that followed, many monuments would be erected in the North and South. By the turn of the century, nearly every courthouse lawn in the eastern United States boasted a memorial to the men from that community who had served. Veterans' groups like the Grand Army of the Republic and the United Confederate Veterans wielded enormous political clout. In 1913, on the fiftieth anniversary of the Battle of Gettysburg, a large reunion was held on the battlefield, with veterans from both sides meeting where Pickett's Charge faltered.

The young men who fought the war eventually became old soldiers. They marched in Decoration Day (later Memorial Day) parades, attended monument dedications and regimental reunions, and took their families to the hallowed battlefields on which they once fought. They frequently met with their one-time opponents, trading stories and forming lifelong friendships based on shared experiences. The last veterans of the Civil War died in the 1950s, nearly a century after its conclusion.

PICKETT'S MEN AT BLOODY ANGLE

A SOLDIER'S TALE

Pictured here is Corporal Alvin B. Williams of Company F, Eleventh Regiment, New Hampshire Volunteers. A native of New London, Williams enlisted as a private on August 11, 1862, at the age of eighteen. He was killed on May 12, 1864, near Spotsylvania Court House. Three weeks earlier, his brother Oscar, also of the Eleventh New Hampshire Volunteers, had died of pneumonia at the Army General Hospital in Annapolis, Maryland. A soldier was more likely to be killed by disease than in action. Estimates of the number of soldiers killed on both sides vary between 620,000 and 750,000, with two-thirds succumbing to disease. Using figures from the 1860 census, 8 percent of all white males between thirteen and forty-three years of age died in the war, proportionately 6 percent in the North and 18 percent in the South.